A Concise Advanced User's Guide to MS-DOS

ALSO AVAILABLE

(By the same author)

A Concise Advanced User's Guide to MS-DOS

by

Noel Kantaris

BERNARD BABANI (publishing) LTD.
THE GRAMPIANS
SHEPHERDS BUSH ROAD
LONDON W6 7NF
ENGLAND

PLEASE NOTE

Although every care has been taken with the production of this book to ensure that any projects, designs, modifications and/or programs, etc., contained herewith, operate in a correct and safe manner and also that any components specified are normally available in Great Britain, the Publishers and Author(s) do not accept responsibility in any way for the failure (including fault in design) of any project, design, modification or program to work correctly or to cause damage to any equipment that it may be connected to or used in conjunction with, or in respect of any other damage or injury that may be so caused, nor do the Publishers accept responsibility in any way for the failure to obtain specified components.

Notice is also given that if equipment that is still under warranty is modified in any way or used or connected with home-built equipment then that warranty may be void.

© 1989, © 1992 BERNARD BABANI (pub.) LTD

First Published - July 1989
Reprinted - March 1990
Reprinted - September 1990
Reprinted - July 1991
Revised Edition - August 1992

British Library Cataloguing in Publication Data:

Kantaris, Noel
    A concise advanced user's guide to MS-DOS
    1. MS-DOS (Computer operating system)
    I. Title
    005.4'469

ISBN 0 85934 209 3

Printed and Bound in Great Britain by Cox & Wyman Ltd, Reading

ABOUT THIS BOOK

This Concise Guide to Advanced MS-DOS has been written for those who already have some knowledge of MS/PC-DOS commands, but who would like to be able to write customised batch files, create specialist programs with the use of the **debug** program and, in general, extend their abilities towards designing and setting up their own professional looking menu screens so that they or others could run any program application or package easily.

The book was not designed to teach you how to use DOS commands in a routine manner. If you need to know about this aspect of DOS, then may I suggest that you refer to either the book *A Concise Introduction to MS-DOS* for pre-DOS 5 users, or the book *A Concise User's Guide to MS-DOS 5* for DOS 5 users, both of which are also published by the Bernard Babani Press. However, in order to also allow this book to be used as a reference guide, a summary of all the commands supported by the MS-DOS 5 operating system is included in the last chapter of the book. The commands are illustrated and explained with relevant examples and, as such, this section of the book can serve as a quick reference guide to the Disc Operating System.

This concise guide was written with the busy person in mind. You don't need to read hundreds of pages to find out most there is to know about a subject, when a few pages can do the same thing quite adequately! With the help of this book, it is hoped that you will be able to get the most out of your computer in terms of efficiency and productivity, and that you will be able to do it in the shortest, most effective and informative way.

ABOUT THE AUTHOR

Graduated in Electrical Engineering at Bristol University and after spending three years in the Electronics Industry in London, took up a Tutorship in Physics at the University of Queensland. Research interests in Ionospheric Physics, led to the degrees of M.E. in Electronics and Ph.D. in Physics. On return to the UK, he took up a Post-Doctoral Research Fellowship in Radio Physics at the University of Leicester, and in 1973 a Senior Lectureship in Engineering at The Camborne School of Mines, Cornwall, where since 1978 he has also assumed the responsibility of Head of Computing.

ACKNOWLEDGEMENTS

I would like to thank colleagues at the Camborne School of Mines for the helpful tips and suggestions which assisted me in the writing of this book.

TRADEMARKS

CONTENTS

1. INTRODUCTION

Most commercial software is designed with 'user-friendly' screens incorporating such screen attributes as reverse video and colour, with information appearing in the right place on the screen. MS-DOS can be utilized to do just that, provided you know how to do it. To this end, you will be shown how to write specialized batch files with the use of the **Edit** screen editor or the **Edlin** line editor, and how to design your own screen menus. You could, of course, buy a commercially available program that could do all this, but then it would cost you a lot and you would not learn anything new.

Which editor you use to write these specialized files depends largely on which version of DOS you are using, with pre-DOS 5 users being restricted to the use of **Edlin**. However, for the sake of completeness, both these editors are fully explained; **Edit** in Appendix A and **Edlin** in Appendix B.

You might already have written batch files to allow you to run an application easily, but creating a professional looking batch file requires you to write some specialised programs in assembler. To this end, you will be shown how to use the **Debug** program to write programs which control the appearance of the cursor, without necessarily having to become an expert assembler programmer. In general, you will be shown how to extend your abilities towards designing and setting up your own professional looking menu screens so that you or others could choose and run program applications or packages easily.

Although the internal DOS commands provide control over the disc drives and, to some lesser extent, control over the keyboard and display screen, the appearance of the latter can be controlled far more effectively with the ANSI.SYS driver, which is an external program supplied with your MS/PC-DOS operating system. Every device that is connected to your computer is controlled by such an external program, usually having the filename extension SYS. However, before any ANSI.SYS command could be used, you must make sure that the path is accessible from the root directory of your system's disc and that the extra line DEVICE=ANSI.SYS is included in the CONFIG.SYS file.

1

If you are not absolutely sure what is meant by the contents of the last paragraph then refer first to the next chapter, entitled 'System Configuration', which was included here for completeness, but might not be of great value to the more experienced DOS user. However, if things are still not clear after you have referred to this section, then perhaps you should refer to either the book *A Concise Introduction to MS-DOS* if you are a pre-DOS 5 user, or the book *A Concise User's Guide to MS-DOS 5* if you are a DOS 5 user, both of which are also published by the Bernard Babani Press, as one of these might be more appropriate for you at this stage with its much lower entry point into DOS.

The ASCII Code of Character Conversion

The ASCII code (which stands for American Standard Code for Information Interchange) is the accepted standard for representing characters in computers. It defines codes 0 to 127; the first 32 (codes 0 to 31) as control characters, which define some action such as line-feed or form-feed, and the remaining (codes 32 to 127) as standard characters which normally appear on a computer keyboard. Since each byte can represent one of 256 possible characters, there are another 128 codes available (codes 128 to 255) for which, however, there is no formal standard laid down. These codes are used by IBM and IBM compatibles and are known as the IBM extended character set.

The IBM extended character set includes four main groups:

a) Accented international characters (codes 128 to 168);
b) Line drawing characters (codes 169 to 223);
c) Greek letters (codes 224 to 239), and
d) Mathematical symbols (codes 240 to 254).

All the codes are shown in the ASCII Conversion Codes table which appears in the following pages. The table shows all 256 characters and tabulates their values in both decimal (base 10) and hexadecimal (base 16) representation. All, but one, ASCII codes can be entered into the computer by holding the key marked <Alt> down and typing the decimal character code on the numeric keypad (not the numbers appearing on the first row of keys of the normal keyboard. On releasing the <Alt> key, the corresponding character appears on the screen. Thus, typing

```
C:\> Alt+236
```

causes the symbol for infinity (∞) to appear on the screen.

The one character code that can not be entered with this method is the 'null' character (code 0). To enter this character, which will appear as ^@ on your screen, press **F7** while at the DOS prompt, or while using **Edlin** or the **Debug** program (the last one of which will be discussed in some detail later). To enter the same character while using **Edit**, first press the Ctrl+P key combination, then press <Esc> followed by the <@> key.

TABLE 1 ASCII Conversion Codes

CHAR	ABBR	DEC	HEX	CHAR	ABBR	DEC	HEX	CHAR	ABBR	DEC	HEX
CTRL @	nul	0	00	CTRL K	vt	11	0B	CTRL V	syn	22	16
CTRL A	soh	1	01	CTRL L	ff	12	0C	CTRL W	etb	23	17
CTRL B	stx	2	02	CTRL M	cr	13	0D	CTRL X	can	24	18
CTRL C	etx	3	03	CTRL N	so	14	0E	CTRL Y	em	25	19
CTRL D	eot	4	04	CTRL O	si	15	0F	CTRL Z	sub	26	1A
CTRL E	enq	5	05	CTRL P	dle	16	10	CTRL [	esc	27	1B
CTRL F	ack	6	06	CTRL Q	dc1	17	11	CTRL \	fs	28	1C
CTRL G	bel	7	07	CTRL R	dc2	18	12	CTRL]	gs	29	1D
CTRL H	bs	8	08	CTRL S	dc3	19	13	CTRL ^	rs	30	1E
CTRL I	ht	9	09	CTRL T	dc4	20	14	CTRL _	us	31	1F
CTRL J	lf	10	0A	CTRL U	nak	21	15				

CHAR	DEC	HEX	CHAR	DEC	HEX	CHAR	DEC	HEX
SPACE	32	20	@	64	40		96	60
!	33	21	A	65	41	a	97	61
"	34	22	B	66	42	b	98	62
#	35	23	C	67	43	c	99	63
$	36	24	D	68	44	d	100	64
%	37	25	E	69	45	e	101	65
&	38	26	F	70	46	f	102	66
'	39	27	G	71	47	g	103	67
(	40	28	H	72	48	h	104	68
)	41	29	I	73	49	i	105	69
*	42	2A	J	74	4A	j	106	6A
+	43	2B	K	75	4B	k	107	6B
,	44	2C	L	76	4C	l	108	6C
-	45	2D	M	77	4D	m	109	6D
.	46	2E	N	78	4E	n	110	6E
/	47	2F	O	79	4F	o	111	6F
0	48	30	P	80	50	p	112	70
1	49	31	Q	81	51	q	113	71
2	50	32	R	82	52	r	114	72
3	51	33	S	83	53	s	115	73
4	52	34	T	84	54	t	116	74
5	53	35	U	85	55	u	117	75
6	54	36	V	86	56	v	118	76
7	55	37	W	87	57	w	119	77
8	56	38	X	88	58	x	120	78
9	57	39	Y	89	59	y	121	79
:	58	3A	Z	90	5A	z	122	7A
;	59	3B	[	91	5B	{	123	7B
<	60	3C	\	92	5C	|	124	7C
=	61	3D	]	93	5D	}	125	7D
>	62	3E	^	94	5E		126	7E
?	63	3F	_	95	5F	del	127	7F

TABLE 1 (Contd)

CHAR	DEC	HEX	CHAR	DEC	HEX	CHAR	DEC	HEX
Ç	128	80	½	171	AB	╓	214	D6
ü	129	81	¼	172	AC	╫	215	D7
é	130	82	¡	173	AD	╪	216	D8
â	131	83	«	174	AE	┘	217	D9
ä	132	84	»	175	AF	┌	218	DA
à	133	85	░	176	B0	█	219	DB
å	134	86	▒	177	B1	▄	220	DC
ç	135	87	▓	178	B2	▌	221	DD
ê	136	88	│	179	B3	▐	222	DE
ë	137	89	┤	180	B4	▀	223	DF
è	138	8A	╡	181	B5	α	224	E0
ï	139	8B	╢	182	B6	ß	225	E1
î	140	8C	╖	183	B7	Γ	226	E2
ì	141	8D	╕	184	B8	π	227	E3
Ä	142	8E	╣	185	B9	Σ	228	E4
Å	143	8F	║	186	BA	σ	229	E5
É	144	90	╗	187	BB	µ	230	E6
æ	145	91	╝	188	BC	τ	231	E7
Æ	146	92	╜	189	BD	Φ	232	E8
ô	147	93	╛	190	BE	Θ	233	E9
ö	148	94	┐	191	BF	Ω	234	EA
ò	149	95	└	192	C0	δ	235	EB
û	150	96	┴	193	C1	∞	236	EC
ù	151	97	┬	194	C2	φ	237	ED
ÿ	152	98	├	195	C3	ε	238	EE
Ö	153	99	─	196	C4	∩	239	EF
Ü	154	9A	┼	197	C5	≡	240	F0
¢	155	9B	╞	198	C6	±	241	F1
£	156	9C	╟	199	C7	≥	242	F2
¥	157	9D	╚	200	C8	≤	243	F3
₧	158	9E	╔	201	C9	⌠	244	F4
ƒ	159	9F	╩	202	CA	⌡	245	F5
á	160	A0	╦	203	CB	÷	246	F6
í	161	A1	╠	204	CC	≈	247	F7
ó	162	A2	═	205	CD	°	248	F8
ú	163	A3	╬	206	CE	∙	249	F9
ñ	164	A4	╧	207	CF	·	250	FA
Ñ	165	A5	╨	208	D0	√	251	FB
ª	166	A6	╤	209	D1	ⁿ	252	FC
º	167	A7	╥	210	D2	²	253	FD
¿	168	A8	╙	211	D3	■	254	FE
⌐	169	A9	╘	212	D4		255	FF
¬	170	AA	╒	213	D5			

The first 32 character codes (0 to 31) can also be entered with the <Ctrl> key, as indicated in the ASCII Conversion Codes table. Using this method, however, causes DOS to echo the caret (^) character followed by the corresponding letter on the screen. **Edlin**, like DOS, allows you to enter the control characters with either the <Ctrl> key or the <Alt> key, but always echoes a caret followed by the appropriate letter.

Computers work with the binary representation (base 2), but as this is too difficult to translate, we tend to work in decimal or hexadecimal representation instead. What follows is a short exposé on the representation of numeric data which you need to know about if you are to understand how computers work.

Binary Data Representation

Numeric information is stored in computers in the form of groups of binary digits (bits for short), that is, 0 and 1. For convenience, information is structured in groups of 8 bits (called a byte). Thus, numbers can be represented in direct binary format in which the right-most bit represents 2 to the power of 0; the next one to the left, 2 to the power of 1; the next one, 2 to the power of 2; and so on, until we reach the left-most bit which is 2 to the power of 7 for an 8-bit structure. This can be represented as follows:

$$2^7 + 2^6 + 2^5 + 2^4 + 2^3 + 2^2 + 2^1 + 2^0$$

A binary number can be converted to its equivalent decimal by multiplying the value of the appropriate Ith bit (which can be either 0 or 1) with the result of 2^I. For example, the binary number 0001 0101 is equivalent to:

$$(0*128)+(0*64)+(0*32)+(1*16)+(0*8)+(1*4)+(0*2)+(1*1)=21$$

decimal.

It can easily be shown that with n bits available, integer numbers within the range 0 to (2^n-1) can be represented. Therefore,

4 bits (called a nibble) can represent the range 0-15
8 bits (called a byte) can represent the range 0-255
16 bits (two bytes) can represent the range 0-65535.

Note the special case of 10 binary digits which give a maximum of 1024 decimal numbers (0-1023). We represent this by the symbol K so that a 512K computer has (512*1024-1)= 524,287 memory locations available. The microprocessor of the IBM PC and compatibles is capable of addressing a maximum of 640 Kbytes of memory starting from location 0 and extending to location 655,359. Of these, approximately 600K are available to the user, as RAM memory for running programs or packages, with the rest being used by the system itself.

Hexadecimal Data Representation

Most operations done by the computer are carried out in binary and although this is easily understood by the computer it causes problems for mere mortals.

For example, the address of memory location 65535 in decimal, is 1111111111111111. Sixteen bits are required to represent all the storage addresses and it is very easy to make mistakes when working with this many digits. The hex numbering system is used to overcome some of these difficulties.

The hex counting system uses base 16 as opposed to base 10 in the decimal and base 2 in the binary system. Counting in 16's is difficult at first, but it does have advantages as you will see later. The value of each column with the different number systems is shown below.

	Value of one unit in column			
	Col 4	Col 3	Col 2	Col 1
Binary	2^3 (8)	2^2 (4)	2^1 (2)	2^0 (1)
Decimal	10^3 (1000)	10^2 (100)	10^1 (10)	10^0 (1)
Hexadecimal	16^3 (4096)	16^2 (256)	16^1 (16)	16^0 (1)

The Hex system requires 16 different digits compared with 10 and 2 in the other systems. It uses 0-9 as in decimal, plus the letters A-F. A list of the first sixteen numbers in each system is listed below:

Binary	Decimal	Hexadecimal
0000	00	0
0001	01	1
0010	02	2
0011	03	3
0100	04	4
0101	05	5
0110	06	6
0111	07	7
1000	08	8
1001	09	9

```
1010          10          A
1011          11          B
1100          12          C
1101          13          D
1110          14          E
1111          15          F
```

An example, converting a hexadecimal number to a decimal number, will make things clearer. The hexadecimal number 0E00 has a decimal equivalent given by

```
  0 (which is decimal  0) * 4096 =    0
+ E (which is decimal 14) *  256 = 3584
+ 0 (which is decimal  0) *   16 =    0
+ 0 (which is decimal  0) *    1 =    0
                                   ────
                                   3584
```

The hexadecimal numbering system has an advantage over binary as one hex digit is equivalent to four binary digits (see Table 2 for conversions). Thus, any 8-bit byte of memory can be represented by two hex digits, and any memory address (which requires twenty binary digits) by five hex digits.

Because of the advantage of hex over both binary and decimal systems, it is used for many computing applications. Although it is not necessary to use the hex system, it is essential to understand it if you are to be able to follow how to use the **Debug** program or want to understand assembly language programming.

TABLE 2 Hex/Binary/Decimal Conversions

Most significant digits

Hex		0	1	2	3	4	5	6	7	8	9	A	B	C	D	E	F
Hex	Bin	0000	0001	0010	0011	0100	0101	0110	0111	1000	1001	1010	1011	1100	1101	1110	1111
0	0000	0	16	32	48	64	80	96	112	128	144	160	176	192	208	224	240
1	0001	1	17	33	49	65	81	97	113	129	145	161	177	193	209	225	241
2	0010	2	18	34	50	66	82	98	114	130	146	162	178	194	210	226	242
3	0011	3	19	35	51	67	83	99	115	131	147	163	179	195	211	227	243
4	0100	4	20	36	52	68	84	100	116	132	148	164	180	196	212	228	244
5	0101	5	21	37	53	69	85	101	117	133	149	165	181	197	213	229	245
6	0110	6	22	38	54	70	86	102	118	134	150	166	182	198	214	230	246
7	0111	7	23	39	55	71	87	103	119	135	151	167	183	199	215	231	247
8	1000	8	24	40	56	72	88	104	120	136	152	168	184	200	216	232	248
9	1001	9	25	41	57	73	89	105	121	137	153	169	185	201	217	233	249
A	1010	10	26	42	58	74	90	106	122	138	154	170	186	202	218	234	250
B	1011	11	27	43	59	75	91	107	123	139	155	171	187	203	219	235	251
C	1100	12	28	44	60	76	92	108	124	140	156	172	188	204	220	236	252
D	1101	13	29	45	61	77	93	109	125	141	157	173	189	205	221	237	253
E	1110	14	30	46	62	78	94	110	126	142	158	174	190	206	222	238	254
F	1111	15	31	47	63	79	95	111	127	143	159	175	191	207	223	239	255

Least significant digits

2. SYSTEM CONFIGURATION

If you are using a hard disc, then it is assumed that you have structured it in such a way as to hold all the DOS external command files in the subdirectory \DOS, all the batch files in the subdirectory \BATCH, and that you would like to hold all the utility programs we develop in this book, in a subdirectory called \UTILS. This supposition is reflected in the full filespec given for ANSI.SYS within the configuration file and the PATH command within the **autoexec.bat** file.

The CONFIG.SYS File

This file allows you to configure your computer to your needs, as commands held in it are executed during boot-up. The easiest way to create or amend this system file is with the use of the full screen editor **Edit** for DOS 5 users (see Appendix A), or the line editor **Edlin** for pre-DOS 5 users (see Appendix B).

DOS 5 Users:

Use the **Edit** screen editor to amend your **config.sys** file so as to include the commands shown overleaf. Again, it is more than likely that your **config.sys** file will include additional commands to those shown below, particularly if you are running a computer with a 386 or higher processor.

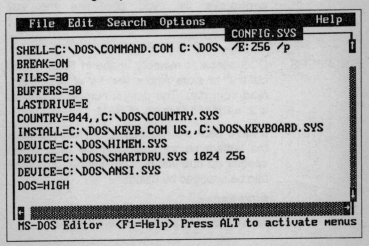

```
 File  Edit  Search  Options                      Help
                                    CONFIG.SYS
 SHELL=C:\DOS\COMMAND.COM C:\DOS\ /E:256 /p
 BREAK=ON
 FILES=30
 BUFFERS=30
 LASTDRIVE=E
 COUNTRY=044,,C:\DOS\COUNTRY.SYS
 INSTALL=C:\DOS\KEYB.COM US,,C:\DOS\KEYBOARD.SYS
 DEVICE=C:\DOS\HIMEM.SYS
 DEVICE=C:\DOS\SMARTDRV.SYS 1024 256
 DEVICE=C:\DOS\ANSI.SYS
 DOS=HIGH


 MS-DOS Editor  <F1=Help> Press ALT to activate menus
```

Pre-DOS 5 Users:
Use the **Edlin** line editor to amend your **config.sys** file so as to include the following commands:

```
1:*FILES=20
2:*BUFFERS=30
3:*BREAK=ON
4:*COUNTRY=044
5:*DEVICE=C:\DOS\ANSI.SYS
```

Users of MS/PC-DOS 3.3 or 4.01, should substitute the following COUNTRY= entry

```
COUNTRY=044,437,C:\DOS\COUNTRY.SYS
```

for the one given above. It is understood, of course, that your particular **config.sys** file might contain additional entries.

Configuration Commands:
The list below, contains commands that you can include within the **config.sys** file. However, do remember that any changes made to this file only take effect after re-booting which can be achieved by pressing the three keys marked Ctrl, Alt and Del simultaneously.

BREAK   By including the command BREAK=ON in the **config.sys** file, you can use the key combination Ctrl+C or Ctr+Break, to interrupt DOS I/O functions.

BUFFERS   DOS allocates memory space in RAM, called buffers, to store whole sectors of data being read from disc. The default number of buffers is 2, each of 512 bytes of RAM.

If more data are required, DOS first searches the buffers before searching the disc, which speeds up operations. The number of buffers can be changed by using:

BUFFERS=n

where n can be a number from 1 to 99.

However, as each buffer requires an additional 0.5 Kbytes of RAM, the number you should use is dependent on the relative size between the package you are using and your computer's RAM. Best results are obtained by choosing between 10-30 buffers.

CODEPAGE   This command is to be found in PC/MS-DOS versions 3.3 and 4.01. The table that DOS uses to define a character set is called a code page. Thus, include the command

`CODEPAGE=437`

where 437 is the code page definition of pre-3.3 versions of DOS.

COUNTRY   DOS displays dates according to the US format which is month/day/year. To change this to day/month/year, use the command

`COUNTRY=044`

where 044 is for U.K. users.

Non U.K. users can substitute their international telephone country code for the 044. The default value is 001, for the USA.

Users of a hard disc with PC-DOS 3.3 or higher, should enter this statement as

`COUNTRY=044,437,C:\DOS\COUNTRY.SYS`

where 437 is the code page of pre-3.3 versions of DOS and **country.sys** is to be found in the \DOS subdirectory.

DEVICE   DOS includes its own standard device drivers which allow communication with your keyboard, screen and discs. However, these drivers can be extended to allow other devices to be connected by specifying them in the **config.sys** file. Example of these are:

`DEVICE=ANSI.SYS`

which loads alternative screen and keyboard drivers for ANSI support - features of which are required by some commercial software.

DEVICE=SETVER.EXE

which sets the DOS version number that MS-DOS 5 reports to a program. You can use this command at the prompt to display the version table, which lists names of programs and the number of the MS-DOS version with which they are designed to run, or add a program that has not been updated to MS-DOS 5.

DEVICE=MOUSEAnn.SYS

allows the use of specific mouse devices.

DEVICE=VDISK.SYS n

allows you to specify the size n in Kbytes (default 64) of RAM to be used as an extra very fast virtual disc. With computers which have more than 640 Kbytes of RAM, the option /E can be used after n in the command to allocate the specified memory size from the extra area of RAM.

DEVICE=DRIVER.SYS

allows you to connect an external disc drive.

DEVICE=EGA.SYS

provides mouse support for EGA modes.

DEVICE=COMn.SYS

specifies asynchronous drivers for the serial ports, where for n=01 specifies an IBM PC AT COM device, and n=02 specifies an IBM PS/2 COM device.

DEVICEHIGH Loads device drivers into the upper memory area under MS-DOS 5.

DOS   Sets the area of RAM where MS-DOS 5 will be
                    located, and specifies whether to use the
                    upper memory area. The command takes the
                    form:

                    DOS=HIGH

DRIVPARM   Sets characteristics of a disc drive under
                    MS-DOS 5.

FCBS   Specifies the number of FCBs that can be
                    opened concurrently. The command takes the
                    following form:

                    FCBS=x,y

                    where x specifies the total number of files by
                    FCBs, from 1 to 255, that can be opened at
                    any one time (the default value being 4), and y
                    specifies the number of opened files (from
                    1-255) that cannot be closed automatically by
                    DOS if an application tries to open more than x
                    files.

FILES   DOS normally allows 8 files to be opened at a
                    time. However, some software such as
                    relational databases, might require to refer to
                    more files at any given time. To accommodate
                    this, DOS allows you to change this default
                    value by using:

                    FILES=n

                    where n can be a number from 8 to the
                    maximum required by your application which
                    usually is 20, although the maximum allowable
                    is 99.

INSTALL   This command runs a terminate-and-stay-
                    resident (TSR) program, such as FASTOPEN,
                    KEYB, NLSFUNC, or SHARE while MS-DOS
                    reads the **config.sys** file. The command is
                    available under DOS 4.01 or higher, and takes
                    the following form:

INSTALL=filespec[params]

where *params* specifies the optional line to pass to the *filespec* which must be FASTOPEN.EXE, KEYB.EXE, NLSFUNC.EXE or SHARE.EXE.

LASTDRIVE   This command is used if additional drives are to be connected to your system, or you are sharing a hard disc on a network. The command takes the form:

LASTDRIVE=x

where x is a letter from A to Z (default E).

REM   REM followed by any string, allows remarks to be entered in the **config.sys**.

SHELL   Manufacturers of some micros provide a 'front end' or an alternative Command Processor to COMMAND.COM as real-mode command-line processor. To invoke this, the command SHELL must be included within the **config.sys** file. The command takes the form:

SHELL=FRONTEND.COM

where FRONTEND is the name of the alternative Command Processor. The default value of SHELL is COMMAND.COM.

STACKS   Sets the amount of RAM that MS-DOS 5 reserves for processing hardware interrupts.

SWITCHES . Specifies the use of conventional keyboard functions even though an enhanced keyboard is installed. The command is only available under MS-DOS 5.

The COMMAND.COM Processor:
This command starts a new command processor that contains all internal commands. This is loaded into memory in two parts: the resident part and the transient part which can be overwritten

by some programs in which case the resident part can be used to reload the transient part. The command takes the form:

COMMAND [options]

with the following available options:

/E   specifies the environment size in bytes, with a default value of 160 bytes

/P   prohibits COMMAND.COM from exiting to a higher level

/C   executes a following command.

For example, the following statement

```
C:\>COMMAND /C CHKDSK A:
```

which might appear in a program starts a new command processor under the current program, runs the CHKDSK command on the disc in the A: drive, and returns to the first command processor.

The AUTOEXEC.BAT File

This is a special batch file that MS-DOS looks for during the last stages of booting up and if it exists, the commands held in it will be executed. One such command is the KEYB xx which configures keyboards for the appropriate national standard, with xx indicating the country. For the U.K., the command becomes KEYB UK, and you will need to execute it if your keyboard is marked with the double quotes sign on the 2 key and/or the @ sign over the single quotes key and/or the £ sign over the 3 key.

Possible contents of the **autoexec.bat** file are as follows:

```
@ECHO OFF
PATH C:\;C:\DOS;C:\BATCH;C:\UTILS
C:\DOS\APPEND \BATCH
MOUSE
C:\DOS\KEYB UK,437,C:\DOS\KEYBOARD.SYS
PROMPT $P$G
SET TEMP=D:\
ECHO HELLO ... This is your PC using
VER
```

where 437 in the KEYB UK command is the code page of pre-3.3 versions of DOS.

15

As mentioned previously under the COUNTRY section, in PC-DOS 3.3 the extended IBM character set has been changed slightly to accommodate several versions of it by offering several choices on the characters displayed or printed. Each such version is referred to by a specific code page number which defines the character set to be used. If you intend to use any other code page than 437, then you should refer to your DOS reference guide.

Do remember, that any changes made to the **autoexec.bat** file only take effect after typing

```
autoexec
```

at the system prompt, or when re-booting the system by pressing the three keys **Ctrl+Alt+Del** simultaneously.

The ECHO Command:
If in your **autoexec.bat** file you do not include the command

```
@ECHO OFF
```

you will notice that every time you boot up the system, the commands within your **autoexec.bat** file are echoed (displayed) onto the screen.

Users of pre-DOS 3.3 should use instead of the @ECHO OFF, the commands

```
ECHO OFF
CLS
```

in their **autoexec.bat** file.

Following the echo off command, the path, keyboard and prompt commands are executed unseen, until echo is re-activated by executing the ECHO command with a trailing message which is displayed on the screen.

The PATH Command:
It is most desirable to be able to use the MS-DOS external commands from anywhere within the directory tree without having to specify where the commands are kept (in this instance, we have transferred them into the DOS directory). The same could be said for the batch files kept in the BATCH directory, or the utility programs kept in the UTILS directory. This can be achieved by the use of the PATH command.

PATH can only find program files, that is, executable command files with the extension .EXE or .COM, or files that DOS recognises as containing such commands, as is the case with .BAT files; for data files you must use the APPEND command as is explained below.

Note the repeated reference to the C: drive within the PATH command, which allows the path to be correctly set even if the user logs onto a drive other than C:.

The APPEND Command:
It is conceivable that the software packages you will be using, require you to type a specific filename in order to activate them. However, some packages also include a second file (most likely a data file which might contain information about the screen display) which is loaded from the first when its name is typed.

In such a case, in addition to including the directory of the package in the PATH command within the **autoexec.bat** file to point to the particular package, you must also include the name of the directory within the APPEND command, otherwise MS-DOS will search for the second (data) file in the root directory, as its extension will most likely be .SCR or .OVL and will not search for it down the PATH.

However, if the second file of a package is an executable file (a file with a .EXE or .COM extension), then you must use the /**X** switch after its name within the APPEND command.

In the suggested changes to your **autoexec.bat** file, the name of the BATCH directory was included in both the PATH and the APPEND command. This allows you to see the contents of a specific batch file, say those of DOS.BAT (to be discussed in the next section), by simply typing at the C:\> prompt:

```
TYPE dos.bat
```

If you do not include the BATCH directory in the APPEND command, MS-DOS will not be able to find the file, unless you specify its directory after the TYPE command. Yet when you type at the C:\> prompt:

```
dos
```

MS-DOS searches down the path, finds the file, recognises it as being a file which contains MS-DOS commands (having the .BAT extension), and executes it.

The APPEND command must be included within the **autoexec.bat** file in a position after the PATH command.

Other commands within the **autoexec.bat** file carry out the following functions:

Command	*Function*
VERIFY	Turns on/off verification that files are written correctly to disc.
GRAPHICS	Allows MS-DOS to print on a graphics printer the information appearing on the screen. The parameter GRAPHICS indicates that printer is either an IBM Personal Graphics Printer, an IBM Proprinter, or an IBM Quietwriter printer.
MOUSE	Loads the mouse driver that comes with the mouse device.
KEYB	Identifies the type of keyboard connected to your system.
PROMPT	Changes the appearance of the MS-DOS command prompt. The parameter $P forces the display of the current drive and path, while the parameter &G displays the greater-than sign (>).
SET	Allows an environment variable named TEMP to be associated with the string C:\WINDOWS\TEMP. This is the subdirectory where Microsoft Windows creates and later deletes temporary files.
VER	Displays the version of MS-DOS running on your system.

A complete summary of all MS-DOS commands is given in the last chapter of this book.

Simple Batch Files

Normally, to complete the implementation of your system's hard disc, you need to create a few batch files in a special subdirectory which you might call \BATCH and which will help to run the system efficiently (if you use a \BATCH subdirectory, you must change the PATH command in the **autoexec.bat** file to include the \BATCH subdirectory as discussed previously). For example, you might require to know the exact name of a DOS command. This can be achieved by creating a batch file to display the contents of the DOS subdirectory, whenever the word **dos** is typed. An example of such a batch file (which we will call **dos.bat**), is:

```
@ECHO OFF
CD \DOS
DIR/P
CD \
```

In the second line, the directory is changed to that of \DOS and the third line causes the contents of the \DOS subdirectory to be displayed using the paging (/P) option. Finally, the fourth line returns the system back to the root directory. Thus, typing **dos**, displays the \DOS subdirectory, while typing any external DOS command, invokes the appropriate command, provided the \DOS subdirectory is included in the PATH.

Finally, it would be ideal if the language BASIC could be accessed direct from the root directory. However, we can not include a \BASIC subdirectory in the PATH command of the **autoexec.bat** file, as we have done with the \DOS directory, because you might have several versions of the Basic language. For example, two such versions were included in the IBM PC-DOS System disc (BASIC and BASICA; A for advanced), while GWBASIC (which is the implementation of the language for use with the compatibles) was included with pre-DOS 5 versions. MS-DOS 5 includes a superior version of Basic which is a sub-set of Microsoft's QBasic. Apart from the above versions, you might also have BBCBASIC - a version of BBC-Basic which runs on the IBM and compatible machines.

We can create a rather special batch file, in the \BATCH subdirectory, to access any of these Basic interpreters, provided they are all in the same \BASIC subdirectory, with the following commands in a batch file which we shall call **bas.bat**

```
@ECHO OFF
CD \BASIC
%1
CD \
```

Note the variable %1 in line 4: which can take the name of any of the Basic languages mentioned above, provided the appropriate name is typed after the batch file name.

For example, typing

```
C:\> BAS QBASIC
```

at the prompt, starts executing the commands within the batch file **bas.bat**, but substituting QBASIC for the %1 variable.

Thus, line 4: causes entry into QBASIC, provided it exists in the BASIC directory. Similarly, typing

```
C:\> BAS GWBASIC
```

causes entry into GWBASIC. Alternatively, we could use named parameters in batch files which allow definition of replaceable parameters by name instead of by number.

To identify named parameters, we use two percent signs, as follows:

```
%BASTYPE%
```

We can use the SET command to define the named parameter. For example, the command

```
SET BASTYPE=QBASIC
```

replaces the %BASTYPE% parameter by the filename QBASIC. The SET command can be used either before the batch file is run, or it can be included within the batch file itself. Thus, the DOS environment variables can be defined as named parameters in a batch file to allow different environments for different applications.

Special Batch-file Commands

Apart from the DOS commands, there are some specific commands which can only be used for batch-file processing. These are presented overleaf.

Command	*Action*
CALL	Allows you to call one batch file from within another. The general form of the command is:

CALL filespec

where *filespec* specifies the drive, subdirectory and name of the batch file to be called. This file must have the extension **.bat**, but must not be included in the filespec part of the CALL command.

The command is used to call a batch file from another batch file.

In the case of pre-v3.3 of DOS, the CALL command can only be used as the last statement of the current file to call another batch file. Return to the first batch file is not possible.

In the case of DOS v3.3 and later, the CALL command can be issued from any place within the current batch file to pass control and execute another batch file. On termination of the called batch file, execution control returns to the calling batch file at the command following the CALL command.

Pipes and redirection symbols must not be used with the CALL command. Batch files that require replaceable parameters can be CALLed. The CALL command can be used to call the current batch file, but care must be taken to eventually terminate execution of the batch file.

ECHO   Enables or disables the screen display of MS-DOS commands which are being executed from within a batch file, or displays the message that follows ECHO.

FOR	Repeats the specified MS-DOS command for each 'variable' in the specified 'set of items'. The general form of the command is:

FOR %%variable IN (set of items) DO command

where *command* can include any DOS command or a reference to the %%var. For example,

FOR %%X IN (F.OLD F.NEW) DO TYPE %%X

will display F.OLD followed by F.NEW.

GOTO label	Transfers control to the line which contains the specified label. For example,

GOTO end

:end

sends program control to the :end label.

IF	Allows conditional command execution. The general form of the command is:

IF [NOT] condition command

where *condition* can be one of

EXIST filespec
string1==string2
ERRORLEVEL=n

Each of these can be made into a negative condition with the use of the NOT after the IF command.

PAUSE	Suspends execution of the batch file.
REM	Displays comments which follow the REM statement.
SHIFT	Allows batch files to use more than 10 replaceable parameters in batch file processing. An example of this is as follows:

```
@echo off
:begin
TYPE %1 | MORE
PAUSE
SHIFT
IF EXIST %1 GOTO begin
```

If we call this batch file **display.bat**, then we could look at several different files in succession by simply typing

display file1 file2 file3

as the SHIFT command causes each to be taken in turn.

The System Environment:

The environment is controlled by 'environment variables' which have names and values allocated to them. The SET command can be used to display, change or delete these environment variables. SET typed without parameters displays the current environment. In our case, typing

```
C:\>SET
```

at the prompt will evoke the response

```
COMSPEC=C:\COMMAND.COM
PATH=C:\;C:DOS;C:\BATCH;C:\UTILS
PROMPT=$P$G
```

COMSPEC shows which Command Processor is being used by the system, while PATH and PROMPT display the corresponding commands in your **autoexec.bat** file.

Some software packages require you to SET environment variables to their specifications if the package is to work correctly. However, since there is a limited amount of space allocated to the environment by DOS, space held by these variables in the environment must be freed. This is achieved by typing SET followed by the environment variable and the = sign. For example, to free the environment of the prompt variable we would use SET PROMPT=.

The space put aside by DOS for the environment is 160 bytes initially, but it is then expanded as you define a command path, a system prompt, or create more environment variables, up to a

23

theoretical maximum of just under 1K bytes for DOS v3.0 and v3.1 or 32K bytes for v3.2. However, this environment expansion only takes place if the SET command is used at the command line. If you use an **autoexec.bat** file to set these variables, then the environment is limited to 160 bytes and attempts to increase the number of directories, say, in the PATH command or load memory resident programs, would cause DOS to display the message 'Out of environment space'.

The size of the environment can be increased for MS/PC-DOS v3.0 and later, with the use of the SHELL= configuration command which must be inserted in the **config.sys** file. The general form of the command is:

```
SHELL=\DOS\COMMAND.COM /E:size /P
```

where

\DOS   is the subdirectory in which the COMMAND.COM
         file can be found,
/E:size is the environment size, and
/P   specifies that the shell is to be permanent.

The actual 'size' must be written in multiples of 16 bytes, if you are using MS/PC-DOS v3.0 or v3.1 (with a maximum value of 62), or directly in bytes, if you are using v3.2 and later (with a maximum value of 32768).

Environment variables can be used in a batch file to represent the variables' value, provided the environment variable is enclosed in percent signs (i.e. %PATH%).

For example, typing at the command line

```
FOR %N IN (%PATH%) DO ECHO %N
```

will produce the output

```
C:\
C:\DOS
C:\BATCH
C:\UTILS
```

on the screen. If you intend to include the above line in a batch file, remember that you need to include two percent signs before N (i.e. %%N) in both occurrences in the FOR statement.

As an example of this, let us write a batch file which will display the contents of the **autoexec.bat** and **config.sys** files on the screen. This can, of course, be achieved by using the **type** command at the prompt and specifying the name of each file individually. To achieve the same thing, use either **Edit** or **Edlin** to create a **show.bat** file in the \BATCH directory, as follows:

```
CLS
FOR %%N IN (\CONFIG.SYS \AUTOEXEC.BAT) DO
TYPE %%N
@ECHO OFF
CD\
```

which, from now on, when you type **show.bat**, displays the following information on your screen:

```
C:\>FOR %N IN (\CONFIG.SYS \AUTOEXEC.BAT)
DO TYPE %N

C:\>TYPE \CONFIG.SYS
FILES = 20
BUFFERS = 30
BREAK ON
COUNTRY=044,437,C:\DOS\COUNTRY.SYS
DEVICE=C:\DOS\ANSI.SYS

C:\>TYPE \AUTOEXEC.BAT
@ECHO OFF
PATH C:\;C:\DOS;C:\BATCH;C:\UTILS
C:\DOS\APPEND \BATCH
MOUSE
C:\DOS\KEYB UK,437,C:\DOS\KEYBOARD.SYS
PROMPT $P$G
SET TEMP=D:\
ECHO HELLO ... This is your PC using
VER
```

The contents of these two files might differ considerably from those of your system, particularly if you are using MS-DOS 5 on a 386 computer with 1 Mbyte of RAM.

3. CONTROLLING YOUR SYSTEM

Overview of ANSI.SYS Commands

ANSI.SYS display commands can be used to position the cursor on any part of the screen, change the intensity of the displayed characters, change their colour, or clear part or all of the screen. ANSI.SYS keyboard commands can be used to re-define keys. For example, you could re-define the function keys so that when you press one a complete command is issued as if it was typed at the keyboard.

ANSI.SYS commands are also called 'escape sequences' because they all begin with the ESCape character (code 27) followed by a left square bracket ([). Commands can also include a numeric or alphabetic code, and each command ends with a different letter. The general form of the command is written as:

```
ESC[<code><letter>
```

where the <code> is a numeric or string value and the ending <letter> identifies the command and is case sensitive (that is, H has a different meaning to h, the former identifying the command that moves the cursor, while the latter sets the display mode). Sometimes, the <code> value might be more than one number or string, in which case it is separated by semi-colons. For example,

```
ESC[2J
```

clears the screen, while

```
ESC[2;35H
```

moves the cursor to the 2nd row and 35th column.

ANSI.SYS commands cannot be typed directly into the keyboard because on receiving the ESCape code, MS-DOS cancels the command. Instead, a text editor, such as **Edit** or **Edlin**, has to be used to create a file with the ESCape codes inserted in command lines. The ANSI.SYS commands in the file can then be sent to the console with the use of the ECHO command, or the entire contents of the file can be displayed with the use of the **type** command.

These commands, and the way they are inserted into **Edit** or **Edlin**, will be discussed fully now.

The ANSI.SYS Console Commands

The ANSI.SYS commands for controlling the console (display and keyboard) fall into four groups. The first three of these have to do with the control of the display, while the fourth deals with the control of the keyboard. They are:

- (a) Cursor control commands,
- (b) Erase display commands,
- (c) Attribute and mode commands, and
- (d) Keyboard control commands.

What follows is a complete summary of all ANSI.SYS console commands appearing under their appropriate category. Each command starts with ESC[(the ESCape character-code 27, followed by a left bracket). The general form of the command is:

```
ESC[<code><letter>
```

where <code> is a string or numeric value (if more than one, they are separated by semi-colons) which identifies the display attribute, display mode, column or row number (or both) to which the cursor is to be moved, the string to be produced when a key is pressed, or the key to be defined. The ending <letter> identifies the command and is case sensitive.

Cursor Control Commands:

===

Cursor Position   ESC[#;#H or ESC[#;#f

Moves the cursor to the specified position. The first # specifies the row (1-25), while the second # specifies the column (1-80) to which the cursor is to be moved. If either the row or column is omitted, their default value, which is 1, is taken.

To omit row, but specify column, the semi-colon must follow the left bracket. If both row and column are omitted then the cursor moves to the home position which is the upper left corner of the screen.

28

Cursor Up	**ESC[#A**
	Moves the cursor up without changing column. The value of # specifies the number of rows by which the cursor is to move up. If the cursor is on the first row, the sequence is ignored. The default value is 1.
Cursor Down	**ESC[#B**
	Moves the cursor down without changing column. The value of # specifies the number of rows by which the cursor is to move down. If the cursor is on the last row, the sequence is ignored. The default value is 1.
Cursor Right	**ESC[#C**
	Moves the cursor to the right without changing rows. If the cursor is on the last column, the sequence is ignored. The default value is 1.
Cursor Left	**ESC[#D**
	Moves the cursor to the left without changing rows. If the cursor is on the first column, the sequence is ignored. The default value is 1.
Save Cursor Position	**ESC[s**
	Saves the current cursor position. The cursor can be moved to this position later with a Restore Cursor Position command.

Restore Cursor Position ESC[u

Restores the cursor position to the value it had when it was last saved with the Save Cursor Position command.

Cursor Position Report   ESC[#;#R

Reports the current cursor position to the standard input device. The first # specifies the current row, while the second # specifies the current column.

Device Status Report   ESC[6n

When this command is received, the console driver outputs a Cursor Position Report sequence.

Erase Display Commands:

===

Erase Display   ESC[2J

Erases the screen and moves the cursor to the home position.

Erase Line   ESC[K

Erases all text from the current cursor position to the end of the line.

Attribute and Mode Commands:

===

Set Attribute   ESC[#;...;#m

Turns on a display attribute. More than one attribute can be specified provided they are separated by semi-colons.

30

Omitting the value of attribute is equivalent to specifying attribute 0, which turns off all attributes.

Attribute parameter numbers can be any of the following:

Attribute	Colour	Foregrd	Backgrd
0 None	Black	30	40
1 Bold	Red	31	41
4 Underline	Green	32	42
5 Blink	Yellow	33	43
7 Inverse	Blue	34	44
8 Invisible	Magenta	35	45
	Cyan	36	46
	White	37	47

Set Display Mode   ESC[=#h

Changes the screen mode and allows line wrap at the 80th column.

A mode parameter number can be one of the following:

Param	Mode
0	40x25 b&w
1	40x25 colour on
2	80x25 b&w
3	80x25 colour on
4	320x200 graphics, colour on
5	320x200 graphics, b&w
6	640x200 graphics, b&w
7	Turn on wrap at end of line

Reset Display Mode   ESC[=#l

The reset mode parameter numbers are the same as those for the Set Display Mode, except that parameter number 7 resets the wrap at the end of a line mode. The l is a lower case letter L.

Keyboard Control Commands:

==

Define Key   ESC[#;...;#p

Assigns one or more characters to be produced when a specified key is pressed. The first # specifies the key to be defined, provided the key is one of the standard ASCII characters with a number from 1 to 127. If the key is a function key, keypad key or a combination of Shift+, Ctrl+ or Alt+key and some other key, then two numbers are required separated by a semi-colon, the first of which is always 0 and the second taken from the table overleaf.

The last # is the character or characters to be produced when a key is pressed. It can be defined as an ASCII code, an extended key code, a string enclosed in double quotes, or any combination of codes and strings separated by semi-colons.

Example:

ESC[0;68;"dir | sort | more";13p

re-defines the F10 key so that the directory command is first piped to a sort command, then to a more command, followed by a carriage return.

To restore a key to its original meaning, enter a Define Key command sequence that sets the last # equal to the first #.

Example:

ESC[0;68;0;68p

restores F10 to its original meaning.

Extended Key Codes:

The extended key codes used with the ANSI.SYS Define Key command are shown below. Each key can be pressed 'alone', or with the <Shift>, <Ctrl> or <Alt> keys. A long dash is used in the table to indicate that the key cannot be re-defined.

TABLE 3 Extended Codes - Standard ASCII Characters

===

Key	Alone	Shift+	Ctrl+	Alt+
Tab	9	0;15	–	–
-	45	95	–	0;130
0	48	41	–	0;129
1	49	33	–	0;120
2	50	64	–	0;121
3	51	35	–	0;122
4	52	36	–	0;123
5	53	37	–	0;124
6	54	94	–	0;125
7	55	38	–	0;126
8	56	42	–	0;127
9	57	40	–	0;128
=	61	43	–	0;131
a	97	65	1	0;30
b	98	66	2	0;48
c	99	67	3	0;46
d	100	68	4	0;32
e	101	69	5	0;18
f	102	70	6	0;33
g	103	71	7	0;34
h	104	72	8	0;35
i	105	73	9	0;23
j	106	74	10	0;36
k	107	75	11	0;37
l	108	76	12	0;38
m	109	77	13	0;50
n	110	78	14	0;49
o	111	79	15	0;24
p	112	80	16	0;25
q	113	81	17	0;16

r	114	82	18	0;19
s	115	83	19	0;31
t	116	84	20	0;20
u	117	85	21	0;22
v	118	86	22	0;47
w	119	87	23	0;17
x	120	88	24	0;45
y	121	89	25	0;21
z	122	90	26	0;44

Extended Codes - Function and Numeric-keypad Keys

Key	Alone	Shift+	Ctrl+	Alt+
F1	0;59	0;84	0;94	0;104
F2	0;60	0;85	0;95	0;105
F3	0;61	0;86	0;96	0;106
F4	0;62	0;87	0;97	0;107
F5	0;63	0;88	0;98	0;108
F6	0;64	0;89	0;99	0;109
F7	0;65	0;90	0;100	0;110
F8	0;66	0;91	0;101	0;111
F9	0;67	0;92	0;102	0;112
F10	0;68	0;93	0;103	0;113
Home	0;71	55	0;119	–
CurUp	0;72	56	–	–
PgUp	0;73	57	0;132	–
CurLft	0;75	52	0;115	–
CurRgt	0;77	54	0;116	–
End	0;79	49	0;117	–
CurDn	0;80	50	–	–
PgDn	0;81	51	0;118	–
Ins	0;82	48	–	–
Del	0;83	46	–	–
PrtSc	–	–	0;114	–

Using Edit to Enter ESCape Commands:

The screen editor **Edit** can be used to enter ESCape command
sequences into a file. The **ESC** character (ASCII 27) is entered

by first typing **Ctrl+P**, then press the <Esc> key which causes
the left arrow (←) to appear on the screen. Thus, to enter

```
ESC[2J
```

which is the ESCape sequence for 'clear screen', evoke **Edit**
and type the appropriate character sequence, as shown below:

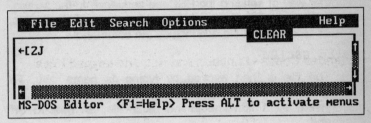

Using Edlin to Enter ESCape Commands:
You can use the **Edlin** line editor to enter ESCape command
sequences into a file. The **ESC** character (ASCII 27) is entered
by typing **Ctrl+V** (displays as ^V) followed by [.
Thus, to enter

```
ESC[2J
```

which is the ESCape sequence for 'clear screen', evoke **Edlin**
and type the appropriate character sequence, as follows:

```
C:\UTILS\> edlin clear
New file
*1i
        1:*^V[[2J
        2:*^C
*e
C:\UTILS\>_
```

You must type two [[, one as part of the ESCape character and
the other as required by the ESC[sequence.

Note: If you use the **Edlin l** (list) command, you will notice that
the ^V[[ESCape sequence has been changed to either [^[(if
you are using MS/PC-DOS v3.0 & v3.1), or ^[[(if you are using
MS/PC-DOS v3.3 and above).

To send the ESCape sequence to the display and, in this case, clear the screen, we must use the **type** command as follows:

```
type clear
```

which clears the screen and causes the prompt to reappear on the second row of the display.

Another way of sending the ESCape sequence to the screen, is from within a batch file using the **echo** command. To do this, we must create a **.bat** file and include the command

```
echo ESC[2J
```

in it. The file is then evoked by typing its name only. To eliminate the second prompt which appears on the screen, you must insert, as a first line in the batch file, an **@echo off** command.

One advantage of using the **type** command to send the ESCape sequence to the display, is that it is instantaneous. The **echo** method can be very slow, particularly if an elaborate screen is to be built up. For this reason, we shall use the former technique for elaborate screens, and in order to avoid having to type the **type** command, we will write a batch file, say **menu.bat**, which contains the entry **type clear**. Thus, typing **menu** evokes the **menu.bat** file which in turn 'types' the contents of **clear** to the display. Try it. The complete batch file should have the following entries

```
@echo off
type clear
```

which assumes that both the **menu.bat** and the **clear** files are to be found in the \UTILS subdirectory. Remember, however, that each time you design a new screen file, the third line of the above batch file has to be changed to use the name of the newest designed screen. You could, of course, make this general by using **type %1**, which however will require you to provide the screen filename after **menu**. The choice is yours.

We are now in a position to start writing some sample files to provide a simple screen menu design. To do this, you must use either **Edit** or **Edlin,** as explained previously to enter the ESCape code sequences. As a first attempt, type in the following, where ESC appears in curly (**{ }**) brackets to make identification easier, and call the file **screen1**.

```
{ESC}[2J
{ESC}[1;30H{ESC}[7mAVAILABLE PACKAGES{ESC}[m
{ESC}[3;2H{ESC}[7m1{ESC}[m Basic
{ESC}[9;2H{ESC}[7m4{ESC}[m Turbo C
{ESC}[7;2H{ESC}[7m3{ESC}[m Q&A
{ESC}[5;2H{ESC}[7m2{ESC}[m Lotus 1-2-3
{ESC}[12;2H{ESC}[7mCHOOSE{ESC}[m
{ESC}[m
```

The above lines perform the following functions:

Line 1	clears the screen;
Line 2	puts the cursor to row 1, column 30; turns on inverse video (attribute 7) and writes 'AVAILABLE PACKAGES'; turns off inverse video (attribute 0);
Line 3 to line 8	write parts of the menu on the screen.

Type in this program carefully, making sure to check each line before running it. If you make mistakes it is possible that you might have to re-boot your computer, as wrong ESCape sequences can cause your computer to hang or do some unexpected things (like blank your screen).

Now, run the program (remember that since no **echo** commands were incorporated in the above file, you will have to use either the command **type screen1** or the generalized form of the **menu.bat** file). If all is well, the following should appear on your screen.

AVAILABLE PACKAGES

1 Basic

2 Turbo C

3 Q&A

4 Lotus 1-2-3

CHOOSE

```
C:\UTILS>_
```

The parts of the menu that appear in bold on paper, will in fact appear in reverse video on the screen. Also, note that the cursor reappears under CHOOSE and, in fact, no choice can be made whatsoever on running this program as it stands.

Two things are immediately obvious from the above program: First, there is no method available to 'respond' in some way to the program, by typing in our choice, test the choice and accordingly branch to the required subdirectory to run the chosen program, and second, we don't have any control over the appearance of the cursor - some method of turning the cursor off and on is required.

To achieve the above we must write three small specialized assembly programs (with the .COM extension) which call for the use of the **Debug** program, which is the subject of the next chapter.

4. THE DEBUG PROGRAM

In order to use the **Debug** program its command file **debug.com** must be in the currently logged directory or there must be a path to it, as the **Debug** program is an external DOS file, in exactly the same way as **Edit** and **Edlin**. If you are using a floppy system, then you will need to copy the **debug.com** file to your working floppy.

Debug can be used to look at memory locations, as well as change such memory locations. It provides a controlled test environment for binary and executable files (files with the .COM or .EXE extension). Here, we first start by looking at memory locations of loaded programs, before venturing further afield. In order to demonstrate how this can be done, we will use a four line **test.txt** file which you should create with the use of either the **Edit** screen editor or the **Edlin** line editor. The file should contain the following lines of text

```
first line of text
second line of text, edited
third line of text
fourth line of text
```

To start **Debug,** type its name followed by the name of the file you want to examine or change. In this case we type

```
C:\UTILS\>debug test.txt
-_
```

provided the file **test.txt** is to be found in the same directory as **Debug**. If it does, it causes **Debug** to respond with its own command prompt, in this case a hyphen (–).

The general form of starting **Debug** is:

debug *filespec arguments*

where *filespec* can be the full file specification, including drive, directory and filename. The *arguments* refer to parameters used by the program you want to examine.

When **Debug** loads a program into memory, it loads it starting at address 0100 hexadecimal (hex 0100, for short) in the lowest available segment. It also loads the number of bytes placed in memory into the CX register (more about this shortly).

39

If the filespec is not given when **Debug** is started, then it is assumed that you want to do one of the following:

(a) Examine current contents of memory,
(b) Load a program into memory using the **Debug Name** or **Load** commands
(c) Load absolute disc sectors into memory with the **Load** command.

The Dump Command

To examine the contents of memory while using **Debug**, type **d** (for dump), followed by 100 (the starting address on which to start the dump) and press <Enter>. This causes the first 128 bytes of memory starting from hex 100 to be displayed on the screen. In our case, the command

```
-d 0100
```

causes the following block to be displayed on the screen:

```
131B:0100  66 69 72 73 74 20 6C 69-6E 65 20 6F 66 20 74 65   first line of te
131B:0110  78 74 0D 0A 73 65 63 6F-6E 65 20 6C 69 6E 65 20   xt..second line
131B:0120  6F 66 20 74 65 78 74 2C-20 65 64 69 74 65 64 0D   of text, edited.
131B:0130  0A 74 68 69 72 64 20 6C-69 6E 65 20 6F 66 20 74   .third line of t
131B:0140  65 78 74 0D 0A 66 6F 75-72 74 68 20 6C 69 6E 65   ext..fourth line
131B:0150  20 6F 66 20 74 65 78 74-0D 0A 0D 0A 74 1C 33 C0    of text....t.3.
131B:0160  F6 86 C2 6F 20 74 09 FF-36 CA 6F 9A A3 76 E0 09   ...o t..6.o..v..
131B:0170  8B F0 E8 5D FD 75 03 96-EB C6 5E C3 8B C7 8B 1E   ...].u....^.....
-
```

Note that information is divided into three main areas:

Address	Byte value in Hex	ASCII characters
XXXX:0100	66 69 72 73 74 20 6C 69-6E 65 20 6F 66 20 74 65	first line of te

where 'address' refers to the address in memory, starting at hex 1DC8:0100 which is shown above as XXXX:0100 because the first part of the address (the XXXX portion of it) broadly defines the location of it in the computer's memory and is dependent on how much memory is installed and on how many resident programs happen to be loaded at the time. This part of the address will, more likely than not, be different on different computers, therefore it is shown above as XXXX.

40

Following the address, there is a block of 16 hexadecimal numbers representing the information held in memory so that location 0100, for example, holds the hex value of 66 (which is the ASCII value of the letter f), while location 0108 (just after the hyphen) holds the hex value of 6E (which is the ASCII value of the letter n). The hyphen here serves to divide the block of 16 bytes in half, for easy location - the first half contains bytes 0 to 7, while the second half contains bytes 8 to 15 inclusive.

The last area of the dump is the ASCII characters contained in the file we happen to be examining. Note that any bytes in that portion of memory having a hex value less than 32 are shown by **Debug** as periods within this last area. Thus, 0D (carriage return - decimal 13) and 0A (line feed - decimal 10) which occur in memory locations 0112 and 0113, respectively, are shown as .. in the second line of the ASCII character portion of the dump. It is worth your while spending some time examining this dump. For example, try to locate the positions of the 'spaces' in the text which have the hex value of 20.

The dump command can also be used without any parameters (i.e. the starting memory location taken as hex 0100 in our previous example). If this had been done the first time we issued the dump command, after starting **Debug**, then dumping would have started at memory location 0100 anyway, as this is the default starting value for a dump of memory. The next time **d** is typed, then the contents of the next 128 bytes of memory are dumped, from hex 0180 to 01FF.

The dump command can also be used to display a specific number of bytes. If this is required, then the command must be followed by the starting and ending address of memory. That is,

    d *start stop*

Thus, to display the first line of our example, you must type

    -d 0100 010F

and press <Enter>.

Another form of the command, in controlling the number of bytes to be displayed, is by specifying the starting location and the length (L) of the required bytes. For example, the first line of our example can be displayed by typing

    -d 0100 L 10

41

In the above command, we used uppercase L to specify length, as the lower-case letter could easily by mistaken as the numeral 1. The number of bytes to be displayed above follows L and is hex 10 which is decimal 16.

The Fill Command
In the dump of the file **test.txt**, we showed the display with certain values after location hex 015A. These values might be different with your computer, because it depends on what happened to be loaded in these locations at the time. We can achieve a more aesthetic result with the use of the **f** (for fill) command. The command takes the following form:

```
-f 0100 0180 0
```

which means 'fill memory locations hex 0100 to 0180 with 0'. Do this and verify it by following it with

```
-d 0100
```

Now all the displayed locations hold the hex value 0 and the ASCII character part of the dump contains only periods.
The general form of the fill command is as follows:

```
f range list
```

If a *range* is specified that contains more bytes than the number of values in the *list*, **Debug** uses the *list* repeatedly until it fills all bytes in the *range*. If the *list* contains more values than the number of bytes in the *range*, **Debug** ignores the extra values in the *list*.

The Load Command
We can now 'load' our **test.txt** file from the buffer into these zeroed locations with the L (for Load) command. Again we use an uppercase letter to avoid confusion by mistaking it for the numeral 1. Thus, typing

```
-L 0100
```

and pressing <Enter>, loads our file from the buffer. To display the result, simply type

```
-d 0100
```

and press <Enter>.

Now you will get a 'cleaner' display of the dump, as the empty memory locations are now filled with 0s.

Note the very last byte of the file in location hex 15A; it contains the value 1A which is what you get when you type **Ctrl+Z**, and represents the end-of-file marker.

The Name Command

The **n** (for name) command is used to assign a filename to **Debug** to use later with the load and write commands. When **Debug** is started without specifying a file, the name command must be used in order to set a file. For example,

```
-n file
-L
```

The name command can also be used to supply a program that is to be used by **Debug** with information essential to its proper execution. For example, we can use the name command to name a file that requires some data by

```
-n file1.com datafile
-L
```

To take up the earlier example of our file **test.txt** and the requirement of an uncluttered display, we can achieve the same thing by simply typing

```
-f 0100 0180 0
-n test.txt
-L 0100
-d 0100
```

causes the following display to appear on your screen:

```
131B:0100  66 69 72 73 74 20 6C 69-6E 65 20 6F 66 20 74 65    first line of te
131B:0110  78 74 0D 0A 73 65 63 6F-6E 64 20 6C 69 6E 65 20    xt..second line
131B:0120  6F 66 20 74 65 78 74 2C-20 65 64 69 74 65 64 0D    of text, edited.
131B:0130  0A 74 68 69 72 64 20 6C-69 6E 65 20 6F 66 20 74    .third line of t
131B:0140  65 78 74 0D 0A 66 6F 75-72 74 68 20 6C 69 6E 65    ext..fourth line
131B:0150  20 6F 66 20 74 65 78 74-0D 0A 0D 0A 00 00 00 00     of text........
131B:0160  00 00 00 00 00 00 00 00-00 00 00 00 00 00 00 00    ................
131B:0170  00 00 00 00 00 00 00 00-00 00 00 00 00 00 00 00    ................
-
```

The Enter Command

The **e** (for name) command allows us to enter data directly into memory as byte values or as a string of characters. The general form of the command is

  e *address list*

where the values in *list* replace the contents of one or more bytes starting at *address*.

Again, assuming that the **test.txt** file has been loaded by **Debug**, we can substitute the existing values in memory starting at address hex 0120 with the string "edited by debug", and display the result, with the following commands:

```
-e 0120 "edited by debug"
-d 0100
```

What is now displayed on your screen is as follows:

```
131B:0100  66 69 72 73 74 20 6C 69-6E 65 20 6F 66 20 74 65   first line of te
131B:0110  78 74 0D 0A 73 65 63 6F-6E 64 20 6C 69 6E 65 20   xt..second line
131B:0120  65 64 69 74 65 64 20 62-79 20 64 65 62 75 67 0D   edited by debug.
131B:0130  0A 74 68 69 72 64 20 6C-69 6E 65 20 6F 66 20 74   .third line of t
131B:0140  65 78 74 0D 0A 66 6F 75-72 74 68 20 6C 69 6E 65   ext..fourth line
131B:0150  20 6F 66 20 74 65 78 74-0D 0A 0D 0A 00 00 00 00    of text........
131B:0160  00 00 00 00 00 00 00 00-00 00 00 00 00 00 00 00   ................
131B:0170  00 00 00 00 00 00 00 00-00 00 00 00 00 00 00 00   ................
-
```

The same changes could be achieved by typing the actual values we want to change in hex. For example, typing

```
-e 0120 65 64 69 74 65 64 20 62 79 20 64 65 62 75 67
```

produces the same change as "edited by debug"!

If the *list* parameter is omitted, then **Debug** displays the address, its contents, and a period, and waits for input.

The Write Command

The **w** (for write) command writes an area of memory to the file was either last loaded by **Debug** or most recently named with the name command. Thus, we can save the changed file of our example above by first naming a file we would like to save the results of the changes in and then writing to that file.

For example, assuming that the **test.txt** file has been changed with the edit command, we could type

```
-n test1.txt
-w
```

which will save the changes in the **test1.txt** file, leaving the old **test.txt** file unaltered.

The general form of the write command is:

w *start*

where *start* is the starting address in memory from which a number of bytes are written to the file. If 'start' is omitted, **Debug** starts at address 0100.

When the write command is executed, **Debug** informs you of the total number of bytes (in hexadecimal) it wrote to the file.

In this case, the message

```
Writing 0005C bytes
```

appears on the screen.

This number is the same as that placed in the CX register when the original file was loaded into memory. In this case, the operation will be correct since we have not changed the actual length of the file. However, had we changed the overall length of the file by, say, appending information to it, then before writing the changes to file, we must change the value held in the CX register to the new length.

Registers

The Intel Central Processing Unit (CPU) family that includes the 8086, 8088, 80x86, are similar in many respects. All these processors can handle 16-bit data internally and can, therefore, accept a common set of instructions. In addition, all these processors communicate with the outside world with a 16-bit data bus, with the exception of the 8088 which operates with an 8-bit data bus, thus making it slower.

The CPUs provide special internal 'memory locations', called registers. For the 8088-80286 CPUs there are 14 such registers each being 16-bits wide, and for the 80386 (or higher) CPUs there are 16, 32-bit registers. Since these registers are integrated within the processor chip, they can manipulate information very quickly. These registers are subdivided into groups according to the tasks they normally perform. The following two tables list the names, length and normal tasks associated with the registers.

TABLE 4 Names and Tasks of 16-bit Registers

15	7	0	
AH	AL		AX, Accumulator
DH	DL		DX, Data
CH	CL		CX, Count
BH	BL		BX, Base
BP			Base Pointer
SI			Source Index
DI			Destination Index
SP			Stack Pointer
CS			Code Segment
DS			Data Segment
SS			Stack Segment
ES			Extra Segment
IP			Instruction Pointer
Flags			Status flags: NV UP EI PL NZ NA PO NC

The first four of the CPU registers are referred to as the general purpose registers AX, BX, CX, and DX. These can be used as either 16-bit or 8-bit registers, which is why they are shown in two halves; the high half (H) and the low half (L). Each half can be addressed separately.

Following the general purpose registers are two pointer and two index registers, which serve as pointers to locate data in main memory. These are referred to as SP (stack pointer), BP (Base pointer), SI (source index), and DI (destination index).

Since all the CPU registers are 16-bits long, this means that any such register can only access 2^{16} = 65,536 (or 64K) bytes of memory. To overcome this limitation, any of these registers can be combined with an appropriate segment register to address much larger chunks of memory, the actual size being dependent on the total number of combined bits.

For example, SS and SP are combined for stack operations, while CS and IP are combined to locate the next instruction. Mostly, these combinations are arranged within the CPU by default. The maximum addressable memory, when two 16-bit registers are combined end-to-end, corresponds to 2^{20} bytes which is one megabyte. Such memory addressing is called the 'effective address'. The segment register is combined with the offset register in the following way.

Suppose that the CS register contains 53C2h and the IP register contains 107Ah, then the physical address will be

```
    53C20h          Segment times 10h (16 decimal)
  +  107Ah          Offset
  -----------------
    54C9Ah
```

Therefore, if the contents of CS and IP were set to address the highest accessible address (0FFFFFh) then CS would contain F000h and IP would contain FFFFh (CS could contain FFFFh and IP contain 000Fh). In other words, there is more than one way of defining a physical memory address.

In the case of the 80386 (or higher) processor, the CPU registers are 32-bits long and addresses may be formed using a 16-bit segment and a 32-bit offset. This gives a maximum possible address space of 2^{48} or a massive 4 gigabytes of memory (this addressing is only permitted when the CPU is operating in 'protected' mode, such as under Microsoft Windows 3.0 or higher and other multitasking environments. A description of this mode of operation is beyond the scope of this book.)

The table on the next page shows the size and general usage of each register in the 80386 (or higher) CPUs.

TABLE 5 Names and Tasks of 32-bit Registers

31	23	15	7	0	
			AH	AL	EAX, Accumulator
			DH	DL	EDX, Data
			CH	CL	ECX, Count
			BH	BL	EBX, Base
			BP		Base Pointer
			SI		Source Index
			DI		Destination Index
			SP		Stack Pointer
			CS		Code Segment
			DS		Data Segment
			SS		Stack Segment
			ES		Extra Segment
			FS		Extra Segment
			GS		Extra Segment
			I P		Instruction Pointer
			Flags		Flags

The Register Command:

The register command allows us to display the names and contents of the registers. To display all the registers, type

```
-r
```

which will cause **Debug** to respond with

48

```
AX=0000  BX=0000  CX=005C  DX=0000  SP=FFEE  BP=0000  SI=0000  DI=0000
DS=131B  ES=131B  SS=131B  CS=131B  IP=0100     NU UP EI PL NZ NA PO NC
131B:0100 66             DB      66
-
```

assuming that file **test1.txt** was in memory at the time. Note the
contents of the CX register which is 005B, the length of our file.

To change the contents of a register, type the register
command, followed by the name of the register. Thus, in the
case of the CX register, type

    -r cx

which causes **Debug** to repeat the name of the register and the
current value held in it (in hex), and then prompt you for a new
value by displaying a colon. For example,

    CX 005C
    :_

At that point we can type the new length of the file in hex.

Appending to a File

As an example, let us add the string "Last line addition" to the
end of the previous file. We start with address 15A which
contains the value 1A representing the Ctrl-Z at the end of the
file. This is not needed and can be overwritten. Thus, typing

    -e 15A "Last line addition"

adds 18 (decimal) bytes to the length of the file which was hex
005B (decimal 91) - look up Table 2 in Introduction for
conversion of decimal to hex, and vice versa.

Since we have already overwritten the contents of location
15A, the new length is 91-1+18 = 108 bytes, occupying
locations 0100 through to 016B. Now add a carriage return (0D)
and a line feed (0A) to the end of the additional line by typing

    -e 016C 0D 0A

which now makes the length to 110 (decimal) bytes or hex 6E.

We now need to change the contents of the CX register, and
to this end we type

    -r cx

which causes **Debug** to display the present contents of the register and prompt for the change, which we type in as 6E, as follows:

```
CX 005C
:6E
```

Before we write the present contents of memory to file, we can name a new file with the **n** command, say **test2.txt**, by typing

```
-n test2.txt
-w
```

which causes **Debug** to respond with

```
Writing 0006E bytes
```

A screen dump of the reloaded file is shown below, which verifies what we have been discussing above.

```
131B:0100  66 69 72 73 74 20 6C 69-6E 65 20 6F 66 20 74 65   first line of te
131B:0110  78 74 0D 0A 73 65 63 6F-6E 64 20 6C 69 6E 65 20   xt..second line
131B:0120  65 64 69 74 65 64 20 62-79 20 64 65 62 75 67 0D   edited by debug.
131B:0130  0A 74 68 69 72 64 20 6C-69 6E 65 20 6F 66 20 74   .third line of t
131B:0140  65 78 74 0D 0A 66 6F 75-72 74 68 20 6C 69 6E 65   ext..fourth line
131B:0150  20 6F 66 20 74 65 78 74-0D 0A 4C 61 73 74 20 6C    of text..Last l
131B:0160  69 6E 65 20 61 64 64 69-74 69 6F 6E 0D 0A 00 00   ine addition....
131B:0170  00 00 00 00 00 00 00 00-00 00 00 00 00 00 00 00   ................
```

The Assemble Command

The general form of the **a** (for assemble) command is

   a *address*

where *address* is the memory location we want to start **Debug** assembling the statement we enter. If the address parameter is omitted, then **Debug** starts assembling with the location following the last location assembled. If the assemble command had not been used since starting **Debug**, the assembling starts with the location pointed to by CS:IP which is CS:0100 if no file is loaded or if the file loaded is a .COM file.

When all statements have been entered, the <Enter> (or <Return>) key must be pressed to provide an empty line which signifies the end location for the assembly.

All numeric values must be entered as 1 to 4 hex digits. Prefix assembler mnemonics must be entered in front of the operation

50

codes (called opcodes) to which they refer, but can also be entered on a separate line. In general, a line of source code is divided into the following four sections:

Label   Mnemonic   Operand   Comment

The 'label' is a symbolic reference to the memory location where the next instruction is located, normally used as the target of a jump or subroutine call. A label can contain alphanumeric characters and the underscore character, but the first character must be a letter. A colon is typed at the end of a label to indicate that this label will be referenced only within the current segment of code.

The 'mnemonic' symbolises a CPU instruction, such as MOV (for move), while the 'operand' refers to the operation to be executed, such as AH,02 (AH referring to the destination, with hex 02 referring to the source).

The 'comment' symbolises an explanation of the instruction and must be preceded by a semi-colon.

Thus, the line

```
begin: MOV AH,02 ; move hex 02 into register AH
```

represents one possible line of assembler instruction.

Below is a list of the mnemonics, together with their meaning, which we will be using later in this book.

TABLE 6 List of Common Assembler Mnemonics

==

ADD	Add destination to source
CMP	Compare destination to source
INT	Call interrupt type
IRET	Interrupt return
JMP	Jump to target
JNZ	Jump if not zero
JZ	Jump if zero
MOV	Move into destination the source

The GO Command

The **g** (for go) command executes the program in memory. Its general form is:

g =address1 address2

where *address1* is the address where **Debug** begins execution and changes both the CS and IP registers, while *address2* sets break-points which stop program execution. If both addresses are omitted, then **Debug** executes the program normally. If the segment is not specified, then **Debug** replaces the value in the IP register with *address1*. The equal sign must be included with *address1*. When program execution reaches a break-point, the **Debug** displays the registers, flags, and decoded instructions of the next instruction ready for execution.

The **go** command uses the IRET instruction to cause a jump to the program under test. When a program is completed, then you must reload the program before you can execute it or debug it again.

The Unassemble Command

The **u** (for unassemble) command, converts memory back to assembly language mnemonics (disassembles bytes) along with address and byte values. The display of a disassembled code looks just like a file ready for assembly. The format is:

u *address*
or
u *range*

where *address* is the address at which disassembly starts with the location pointed to by CS:IP. If *address* is omitted, then **Debug** starts converting code after the last location disassembled. If *range* is omitted, **Debug** disassembles 20 hex bytes.

The Quit Command

The **q** (for quit) command can be used to leave **Debug** and return to DOS without saving any changes made. To save the contents of memory to file, the write command must be issued before the quit command.

There are a lot more commands in **Debug**, but what has been presented here is more than enough for what we need.

5. WRITING IN ASSEMBLY CODE

We shall now use **Debug** to write a few small programs in assembly code which can use DOS directly to produce useful reactions from your computer. You don't need to know how to program in assembler to write these useful utilities, but if you are curious to know what the commands mean, then please refer to Table 1 at the beginning of the book, which lists the ASCII conversion codes, and to Tables 4 and 5 at the end of the previous chapter, which list the respective names of the CPU registers and the assembler mnemonics used in these programs. Interrupts and non-sequential program execution, such as code jumps, are discussed in the next chapter.

It is assumed here that your have configured your system according to the advice given earlier, that is, the command DEVICE=C:\DOS\ANSI.SYS is included in your **config.sys** file, and that PATH=C:\;C:\DOS;C:\BATCH;C:\UTILS is incorporated in your **autoexec.bat** file, if you are using a system with a hard disc. The programs created in this book are saved in the \UTILS subdirectory. If, on the other hand, you would prefer to save all created programs on a floppy in the A: drive, then copy to the floppy the **debug.exe** file from the \DOS subdirectory (**debug.com** if you are a pre-DOS 5 user), and either the **edit.com** and **edit.hlp** files (if you are a DOS 5 user) or the **edlin.com** file (if you are a pre-DOS 5 user). In this way, you can log into either the \UTILS subdirectory, or the A: drive and start writing in assembly code without further references to other drives or subdirectories.

We start by evoking the **Debug** program and typing the commands shown below, as follows:

```
C:\UTILS\>debug
-a 0100
0D43:0100 mov DL,07
0D43:0102 mov AH,02
0D43:0104 int 21
0D43:0106 int 20
0D43:0108 <enter>
-r cx
CX 0000
:08
-n bleep.com
```

53

```
-w
Writing 0008 bytes
-g

Program terminated normally
-q
C:\UTILS\>_
```

Thus, after invoking **Debug**, you type the assemble command

```
a 0100
```

which causes **Debug** to respond with

```
XXXX:0100
```

and wait on the same line for your entries. XXXX above is used to indicate that this part of the address will most certainly by different for your computer as it is dependent on the amount of memory available. At this stage you type the move command

```
mov DL,07
```

which moves hex 07 into register DL. Note that hex 07 from Table 1 is in fact the 'bell'. On pressing <Enter>, **Debug** responds with

```
XXXX:0102
```

and again waits on the same line for your entries. The move command in the second line

```
mov AH,02
```

selects function 2 (which displays a character) of the DOS interrupt 21 hex, itself being selected by the command

```
int 21
```

in the third line. Finally, the interrupt command

```
int 20
```

in the fourth line, calls a special DOS routine to return control from the current program to DOS. Program flow, as well as interrupts and their various functions, will be discussed shortly. However, you don't need to understand their precise function at this stage, in order to understand what we have set out to accomplish.

Finally, the assemble command is terminated by pressing the <Enter> or <Return> key, shown as

```
<enter>
```

in the fifth line.

Before the program can be written to disc, we need to tell **Debug** of its length with the register command

```
r cx
```

which causes **Debug** to inform us that the current length is 0000 bytes and prompts us for an entry to which we should respond by typing the actual length which, in this case, is 08.

Now the program is named **bleep.com** with the name command - it is imperative that the extension **.com** is given to assembly language programs. Then, the program is written to disc with the write command which causes **Debug** to respond with

```
Writing 0008 bytes
```

The **go** command can be issued at this point to find out whether the program actually works as expected. If it does, then **Debug** responds with the message

```
Program terminated normally
```

at which point we can quit **Debug** and can activate the **bleep.com** program by simply typing **bleep**.

However, if you made any mistakes in entering your program into **Debug** it is possible that any number of unexpected things might happen when the **go** command is issued, including no further response from your computer. If this happens, then reset the system and reload into **Debug** the offending program, unassemble it and correct it before saving it and running it again. As an example, we show below what you will see if you use **Debug**'s unassemble command on the **bleep.com** program.

```
-u 0100
0D43:0100 B207          MOV     DL,07
0D43:0102 B402          MOV     AH,02
0D43:0104 CD21          INT     21
0D43:0106 CD20          INT     20
0D43:0108 F6F6          DIV     DH
```

Obviously, **Debug** is not an easy program to use as an editor to correct long programs, even though it is ideal for assembling short ones.

Creating a Script File

A better method of creating long assembly language programs is with the use of either **Edlin** or **Edit** to create what is known as a 'script' file that holds all the information that normally is typed into **Debug**, then activating **Debug** with its input redirected to the script file. As an example, use either **Edit** or **Edlin** as follows:

```
C:\UTILS\>edit bleep.scr
```

or

```
C:\UTILS\>edlin bleep.scr
```

to create the script file of the same **bleep.com** file. The script file should contain the following commands:

```
a   0100
    mov DL,07
    mov AH,02
    int 21
    int 20

r cx
08
n bleep.com
w
q
```

Now save the file and exit the editor. Then, invoke **Debug** by typing

```
C:\UTILS\>debug <bleep.scr
```

which will create the desired program automatically. The response of **Debug** to this re-direction will be:

```
-a  0100
0D43:0100 mov DL,07
0D43:0102 mov AH,02
0D43:0104 int 21
0D43:0106 int 20
0D43:0108
```

```
-r cx
CX 0000
:08
-n bleep.com
-w
Writing 0008 bytes
-q

C:\UTILS\>_
```

In this way, any errors in the program can be put right by first using either **Edit** or **Edlin** to correct the **.scr** file, and then starting **Debug** again with its input redirected to the corrected script file.

Control of Program Flow

The microprocessor is responsible for the correct control of program flow. This is achieved by repeatedly

(a) fetching instructions from memory, and
(b) executing them.

In the absence of any program jumps or calls to subroutines, these instructions are executed sequentially.

A register called the Program Counter (PC) controls which instructions are fetched and at any given time this register contains the memory location holding the instruction being executed. After execution of the first instruction, the microprocessor increments the Program Counter by one and fetches the next instruction to be executed. This process continues until all the instructions in the program are executed.

Non-sequential Program Execution:

The 'jump' instruction performs an unconditional jump in program execution.

An example of this is given below. Start **Debug** in the usual way, then type the following instructions:

```
-f 0100 0200 0
-a 0100
0D43:0100  mov AL,05
0D43:0102  jmp 0106
0D43:0104  mov AL,07
```

```
0D43:0106 mov [0110],AL
0D43:0109
_
```

The program first puts the hex number 05 into the low part of
the AX register (AL), and then program execution jumps
unconditionally to location 0106, thus avoiding the second **mov**
instruction in location 0104. Then, in order to prove that this
jump command has been executed correctly, the instruction in
location 106 forces the contents of the AL register to be copied
into memory address [0110]. Program execution can be started
by typing the **go** command, namely,

```
g =0100 0109.
```

which causes the following to appear on the screen:

```
AX=0005  BX=0000  CX=0000  DX=0000  SP=FFEE  BP=0000  SI=0000  DI=0000
DS=0D43  ES=0D43  SS=0D43  CS=0D43  IP=0109   NU UP EI PL NZ NA PO NC
0D43:0109 0000          ADD      [BX+SI],AL                    DS:0000=CD
-
```

Using Debug's Trace Command:

Debug's **t** (for trace) command is used to execute a program,
instruction by instruction. Thus, typing

```
-t =0100
```

causes **Debug** (if you include the = sign) to display register
information after each trace command, as follows:

```
-t =0100

AX=0005  BX=0000  CX=0000  DX=0000  SP=FFEE  BP=0000  SI=0000  DI=0000
DS=0D43  ES=0D43  SS=0D43  CS=0D43  IP=0102   NU UP EI PL NZ NA PO NC
0D43:0102 EB02          JMP      0106
-t

AX=0005  BX=0000  CX=0000  DX=0000  SP=FFEE  BP=0000  SI=0000  DI=0000
DS=0D43  ES=0D43  SS=0D43  CS=0D43  IP=0106   NU UP EI PL NZ NA PO NC
0D43:0106 A21001          MOV      [0110],AL                   DS:0110=00
-t

AX=0005  BX=0000  CX=0000  DX=0000  SP=FFEE  BP=0000  SI=0000  DI=0000
DS=0D43  ES=0D43  SS=0D43  CS=0D43  IP=0109   NU UP EI PL NZ NA PO NC
0D43:0109 0000          ADD      [BX+SI],AL                    DS:0000=CD
```

In this case, the value 05 is first moved into register AL. The
next instruction is at location 0102 which however forces a jump

to location 0106. The contents of the lower part of the AX register are still holding the value 05.

Finally, to prove that the value 05 has indeed been moved into address 0110, type

```
-d 0100
```

which causes the following display to appear on your screen, showing that value 05 has been moved into location 0110:

```
-d 0100
0D43:0100  B0 05 EB 02 B0 07 A2 10-01 00 00 00 00 00 00 00   ................
0D43:0110  05 00 00 00 00 00 00 00-00 00 00 00 00 00 00 00   ................
0D43:0120  00 00 00 00 00 00 00 00-00 00 00 00 00 00 00 00   ................
0D43:0130  00 00 00 00 00 00 00 00-00 00 00 00 00 00 00 00   ................
0D43:0140  00 00 00 00 00 00 00 00-00 00 00 00 00 00 00 00   ................
0D43:0150  00 00 00 00 00 00 00 00-00 00 00 00 00 00 00 00   ................
0D43:0160  00 00 00 00 00 00 00 00-00 00 00 00 00 00 00 00   ................
0D43:0170  00 00 00 00 00 00 00 00-00 00 00 00 00 00 00 00   ................
-
```

Conditional Program Jumps:

Conditional jumps in program execution can be achieved by first setting the condition and then using the **cmp** (for compare) command. This command compares two parameters and if the difference between them is zero, then a special flag is set. This is the fifth flag shown at the bottom of Table 4, which is marked NZ (for not zero). Flags are registers which have only two states; they either 'set' or 'not set'. The **cmp** command sets the zero flag which then reads ZR (for zero). If the zero flag has not been set, it appears as NZ.

The following example will help the illustrate the above points. Evoke **Debug** and type the following instructions:

```
-f 0100 0200 0
-a 0100
0D43:0100  mov AL,05
0D43:0102  cmp AL,05
0D43:0104  jnz 0108
0D43:0106  mov AL,07
0D43:0108  mov [0110],AL
0D43:010B
```

To see the program execute one instruction at a time, use the trace command as shown overleaf. This will also display the state of the zero flag.

```
AX=0005  BX=0000  CX=0000  DX=0000  SP=FFEE  BP=0000  SI=0000  DI=0000
DS=0D43  ES=0D43  SS=0D43  CS=0D43  IP=0102   NV UP EI PL NZ NA PO NC
0D43:0102 3C05          CMP     AL,05
-t

AX=0005  BX=0000  CX=0000  DX=0000  SP=FFEE  BP=0000  SI=0000  DI=0000
DS=0D43  ES=0D43  SS=0D43  CS=0D43  IP=0104   NV UP EI PL ZR NA PE NC
0D43:0104 7502          JNZ     0108
-t

AX=0005  BX=0000  CX=0000  DX=0000  SP=FFEE  BP=0000  SI=0000  DI=0000
DS=0D43  ES=0D43  SS=0D43  CS=0D43  IP=0106   NV UP EI PL ZR NA PE NC
0D43:0106 B007          MOV     AL,07
-t

AX=0007  BX=0000  CX=0000  DX=0000  SP=FFEE  BP=0000  SI=0000  DI=0000
DS=0D43  ES=0D43  SS=0D43  CS=0D43  IP=0108   NV UP EI PL ZR NA PE NC
0D43:0108 A21001        MOV     [0110],AL                      DS:0110=00
-
```

Note that the zero flag appears as NZ (being not set), immediately after the first trace command which executes the first **mov** command, moving the value 05 into AL. After the second trace command, the zero flag is set and it appears as ZR once the **cmp** command is executed. The IP (instruction pointer) register holds the location of the next executable statement, which in this case confirms that since the result of the comparison is zero and the conditional program jump only takes place if the difference is 'not zero', then the next instruction to be executed is to be found in location 0106 which moves the value 07 into AL. To confirm this, dump the contents of the relevant locations, as follows:

```
-d 0100
0D43:0100  B0 05 3C 05 75 02 B0 07-A2 10 01 00 00 00 00 00   ..<.u..........
0D43:0110  07 00 00 00 00 00 00 00-00 00 00 00 00 00 00 00   ...............
0D43:0120  00 00 00 00 00 00 00 00-00 00 00 00 00 00 00 00   ...............
0D43:0130  00 00 00 00 00 00 00 00-00 00 00 00 00 00 00 00   ...............
0D43:0140  00 00 00 00 00 00 00 00-00 00 00 00 00 00 00 00   ...............
0D43:0150  00 00 00 00 00 00 00 00-00 00 00 00 00 00 00 00   ...............
0D43:0160  00 00 00 00 00 00 00 00-00 00 00 00 00 00 00 00   ...............
0D43:0170  00 00 00 00 00 00 00 00-00 00 00 00 00 00 00 00   ...............
-
```

which shows that value 07 has been moved into location 0110.

Now use **Debug** to change the instruction starting in location 0104, as follows:

```
-a 0104
0D43:0104 jz  0108
0D43:0106
```

and then use the trace command again to confirm that the program will now skip the instruction in location 0106, thus placing the hex value 05 into location 0110.

Interrupts

Interrupts provide a way for I/O devices to communicate with the CPU. An interrupt informs the processor that an external device needs attention, which causes the processor to suspend its current activity and respond to it. On receipt of an interrupt, the processor finishes executing the last instruction, saves the address of the next instruction on the stuck (a special contiguous memory block, the location of which is to be found in the SP (stuck pointer) register), then jumps to the special interrupt handling subroutines which are to be found in certain parts of the computer's memory, executes the appropriate one and returns to the suspended program by fetching the address of the next instruction from the stuck.

The Intel 8088 and 8086 family of processors can address one megabyte of memory by combining a general register with a segment register. Different parts of this memory have been apportioned to different activities with some activities being in ROM (Read Only Memory) and containing permanent instructions for the operation of the computer, while other activities, such as user's programs and their data are held in RAM (Random Access Memory).

The memory map of an IBM PC is shown below with each of the 16 possible different segments containing 64 Kbytes. The address of each 64 Kbyte segment begins with a different hexadecimal digit (0-9) or letter (A-F), with the first two referring to the 64 Kbyte segment, and the second two to the offset within each segment.

TABLE 7 Memory Map of the IBM PC

===

Address	Description
0000	BIOS interrupts
0080	DOS interrupts
0040	BIOS data area
0050	DOS & Basic data area
A800	Enhanced graphics

61

B000	Monochrome adapter
B800	Graphics adapter
C800	Hard Disc ROM
F600	ROM Basic
FE00	ROM BIOS

Memory locations from 0000 to 9FFF, which constitutes 640KB, is allocated as RAM working space. Segments A800, B000 and B800 contain RAM allocated respectively to enhanced-graphics video memory, and the video screens. Segments C800, F600 and FE00, contain ROM and is allocated respectively to the operation of the hard disc, Basic and instructions for the power up self-test and operation of peripherals.

The first 1024 bytes of RAM memory, known as the *interrupt vector table*, contain the 256 interrupt vectors which provide entry points into subroutines residing elsewhere in memory. These subroutines communicate directly with peripherals through registers and their addresses are numbered from 0 to FF. Since these vectors are located in memory, any program can use them to demand service from the appropriate subroutine.

The interrupt vectors are organized under a priority scheme and can be grouped into three basic categories, as follows:

(a) Internal hardware interrupts occupy the lowest part of the 1024 bytes of system memory from hexadecimal 00 to 1F, with interrupt levels running from hex 00 to 0D. These are generated by certain events during program execution, such as encountering an invalid opcode. The assignment of such events to the appropriate interrupt number is wired into the processor and is unmodifiable.

(b) External hardware interrupts occupy certain areas within the first 1024 bytes of system memory other than hex ranges 00 to 1F and 20 to 3F. The external hardware interrupts are triggered by co-processors or controllers of peripheral devices. They are not wired directly to the CPU, but are channelled through a special Program-mable Interrupt Controller device, PIC for short, which is controlled by the CPU through a set of I/O ports. Different peripheral devices are assigned to their corresponding

interrupt levels, the assignment being made by the manufacturers of the equipment and thus being unmodifiable
by software.

(c) Software interrupts can be triggered by any program by
simply issuing the instruction

INT N

where N is the interrupt level number which then
generates a call to the address of the appropriate
subroutine. Interrupts with hexadecimal numbers from 20
to 3F, are used by DOS to communicate with its modules
and with application programs. Other interrupts are used
by the ROM BIOS, by application software for various
purposes, or system drivers. The table below lists the
interrupt vector type and its function.

TABLE 8 Software Interrupt Vectors for the IBM PC

===

Vector	Function
05	Print screen
08	Timer
09	Keyboard scan code
0B	Asynchronous comms port controller 1
0C	Asynchronous comms port controller 0
0D	Hard disc controller
0E	Floppy disc controller
0F	Printer controller
10	Video screen driver
11	Equipment configuration check list
12	Memory size check
13	Hard/Floppy disc driver
14	Serial comms port driver
15	Cassette I/O, AT auxiliary functions
16	Keyboard driver
17	Printer driver
18	ROM Basic
19	Bootstrap loader
1A	Read/Set time clock
1B	Ctrl-Break handler

1C	Timer control
1D	Video parameter table
1E	Disc parameter table
1F	Graphics character table
20	Terminate COM program
21	General DOS services
22	Program terminate code
23	Ctrl+C code
24	Error code
25	Absolute disc read
26	Absolute disc write
27	Terminate but stay resident
28-2E	Reserved for DOS
2F	Print spooler
30-3F	Reserved for DOS
40	Floppy disc driver
41	Hard disc parameter table

The most important DOS interrupt is hex 21 because it performs a number of useful operations. These operations as categorized and are given a 'function' number, as listed below. To use these functions, the function number must be placed in register AH. Once this is done, and other registers are established as required, the command INT 21 is given. On return, data may be available in one or more registers.

TABLE 9 The Functions of DOS Services Interrupt 21

AH value	Function description
00	Terminate program and return to DOS
01	Read and display keyboard input character
02	Write character to video screen
03	Read from serial port
04	Write to serial port
05	Write to printer port
06	Direct keyboard input and video output
07	Read keyboard input without echo or Break detection

08	Read keyboard input without echo but with Break detection
09	Display a string of characters
0A	Read keyboard buffer
0B	Keyboard input status
0C	Reset input buffer and invoke keyboard input
0D-24	Disc operations, but with 18 & 1D-20 reserved
25	Set machine interrupt vector to point to an interrupt handling routine
26	Create program segment prefix
27-29	File operations
2A-2D	Fetch and set system date and time
2E	Set verify flag
2F	Fetch disc transfer area address
30	Fetch DOS version number
31	Terminate but stay resident
32	Reserved
33	Fetch or set Ctrl+Break flag
34	Reserved
35	Fetch interrupt vector
36	Fetch free disc space
37	Reserved
38	Fetch or set country
39-43	File and directory operations
44-47	File and device-driver control information
48	Allocate block of memory
49	Release block of memory
4A	Change size of allocated memory
4B	Load and execute a program
4C	Terminate a program and return to DOS
4D	Fetch return code
4E-5D	File operations, but with 50-53, 55 and 5D reserved
5E	Fetch and set printer set-up
5F-63	Re-direction and address operations, but with 60-61 reserved

---

6. THE FINAL ASSEMBLAGE

Creating Interactive Batch Files

In order to make batch files interactive, we need to create a small program which 'responds' to the keyboard keys most recently pressed. This is a bit similar to the INKEY command in high level computer languages that reads a character from the keyboard.

Normally, when a key is pressed, a code representing that key is sent to DOS for translation and subsequent display. However, DOS also stores the value of this code in a part of memory which can be accessed and is normally referred to as the 'errorlevel'. The key codes of both the standard ASCII and extended ASCII characters were discussed earlier and are listed in Tables 1 and 2, respectively.

Because the first number of the two-number value representing the extended key codes is always 0, DOS sets errorlevel to the second number. This, inevitably produces some duplication between standard and extended key codes (for example, the numeric key 0, Alt+b and Shift+Ins all set errorlevel to 48), but we can put up with it because the keys responsible are unrelated.

To create **respond.com**, evoke either **Edit** or **Edlin** by typing

```
C:\UTILS\>edit respond.scr
```

or

```
C:\UTILS\>edlin respond.scr
```

and create the appropriate script file. The script file should contain the following commands:

```
a  0100
   mov AH,07
   int 21
   cmp AL,00
   jnz 010C
   mov AH,07
   int 21
   mov AH,4C
   int 21

r cx
```

```
10
n respond.com
w
q
```

```
C:\UTILS\>_
```

Now, we can invoke **Debug** by typing

```
C:\UTILS\>debug <respond.scr
```

which will create the desired program automatically.

We can then rewrite the **menu.bat** file (calling it **menu1.bat**) to incorporate the **respond.com** file as follows:

```
@echo off
  type screen1
:GETKEY
  respond
  if errorlevel 53 goto GETKEY
  if not errorlevel 49 goto GETKEY
```

where **screen1** was created earlier in this book, using either **Edit** or **Edlin**, and has the following contents:

```
{ESC}[2J
{ESC}[1;30H{ESC}[7mAVAILABLE PACKAGES{ESC}[m
{ESC}[3;2H{ESC}[7m1{ESC}[m Basic
{ESC}[5;2H{ESC}[7m2{ESC}[m Turbo C
{ESC}[7;2H{ESC}[7m3{ESC}[m Q&A
{ESC}[9;2H{ESC}[7m4{ESC}[m Lotus 1-2-3
{ESC}[12;2H{ESC}[7mCHOOSE{ESC}[m
{ESC}[m
```

On running **menu1.bat** now, we get the following display:

AVAILABLE PACKAGES

1   Basic

2   Turbo C

3   Q&A

4   Lotus 1-2-3

CHOOSE

_

with the cursor appearing under **CHOOSE** rather than next to it. Nevertheless, the program now responds only to inputs 1 to 4 inclusive, which make the prompt reappear.

Note that 'errorlevel' is checked backwards; the first **if** command checks whether 'errorlevel' is greater than or equal to the specified number which, in this case, excludes all codes greater than or equal to 53. The second **if** command in the batch file first checks to see whether 'errorlevel' is greater or equal to 49, but then the 'not' in the statement inverts the logic which now has the effect of checking to see whether 'errorlevel' is less than the specified number, which in this case is 49. In this way the batch file returns command to DOS only if keys 1 to 4 are typed which correspond to key codes 49 to 52 inclusive.

We can improve the batch file **menu1.bat** to actually respond by telling us which key was pressed. To do this, modify the file (calling it **menu2.bat**) to include the following:

```
@echo off
:AGAIN
    type screen1
:GETKEY
    respond
    if errorlevel 53 goto GETKEY
    if errorlevel 52 goto FOURTH
    if errorlevel 51 goto THIRD
    if errorlevel 50 goto SECOND
    if errorlevel 49 goto FIRST
    if errorlevel 48 goto QUIT
    if not errorlevel 48 goto GETKEY
:FOURTH
        echo You have typed 4
        respond
        goto AGAIN
:THIRD
        echo You have typed 3
        respond
        goto AGAIN
:SECOND
        echo You have typed 2
        respond
        goto AGAIN
:FIRST
        echo You have typed 1
```

```
          respond
          goto AGAIN
:QUIT
          cls
          bleep
          echo Bye
```

Now, the batch file responds appropriately to the keys you type, with the 0 (zero) acting as the 'quit' key. Note the use of the **respond** program as a 'pause' command (without the latter's message to the user), which passes control to the **goto** command only after a key (any key) is pressed.

Controlling the Cursor

We can improve the appearance of the previously written menu batch files by incorporating two assembly language programs which control the cursor. The first program is designed to turn the cursor off, so that it does not appear in unwanted areas on the screen, while the second is designed to turn the cursor back on again.

Now use **Edit** or **Edlin** to first write the script file **cursoff.scr**, to turn the cursor off, with the following contents:

```
a  0100
   mov AH.01
   mov CH,20
   int 10
   int 20

r  cx
08
n  cursoff.com
w
q
```

then write the script file **curson.scr**, to turn the cursor on, with the following contents:

```
a  0100
   mov AH,0F
   int 10
   cmp AL,07
   jz  010D
   mov CX,0607
```

```
      jmp 0110
      mov CX,0B0C
      mov AH,01
      int 10
      int 20

   r cx
   16
   n curson.com
   w
   q
```

Now, use **Debug** with its input redirected to the script file **cursoff.scr**, to create the **cursoff.com** program, as follows:

```
C:\UTILS\>debug <cursoff.scr
```

followed by the reactivation of **Debug** with its input redirected to the script file **curson.scr** to create the **curson.com** program.

To demonstrate how these two programs can be used to enhance batch files, edit the contents of the batch file **menu1.bat** (calling it **menu3.bat**) incorporating the following changes:

```
@echo off
   type screen1
   cursoff
:GETKEY
   respond
   if errorlevel 53 goto GETKEY
   if not errorlevel 49 goto GETKEY
   curson
```

On running this batch file, you will see that now the cursor is removed from the screen and does not reappear until you type the correct information. Note that both these programs (as indeed all the programs we have created using **Debug**) can be used by themselves. Thus typing **cursoff** will make the cursor disappear from the screen, while typing **curson** makes it reappear. As an exercise, try to use **cursoff** and **curson** in the **menu2.bat** file. Call the result **menu4.bat**.

Designing a Menu Screen

We can now use all the expertise gathered so far to design a menu screen which is pleasing to the eye. As all the menu titles appear within a boxed area, the box-drawing characters needed for this are given below for convenience, even though they also appear in Table 1.

┌ Alt+201	= Alt+205	┐ Alt+187
╟ Alt+199	− Alt+196	╢ Alt+182
└ Alt+200	‖ Alt+186	┘ Alt+188

Now use **Edit** or **Edlin** to create **screen2**, remembering that the {ESC} part of each line is entered in **Edit** using the ESCape code sequence Ctrl+P, pressing the <Esc> key, followed by the square bracket ([) shown in the text after {ESC}. With **Edlin** you will have to use the ESCape code sequence Ctrl+V[, followed by the square bracket ([) shown in the text after {ESC}. With

Note that line 2 is shown in the text displayed on the next page, foreshortened; it should, in fact, be 29 = characters long before the {ESC} sequence preceding the message, and 30 = characters long after the message. Similarly, at the bottom of the file, the corresponding number of the = character is 30 before and 31 after the message. The number of characters making up the single lines should be 76 each.

```
{ESC}[2J
┌─────────── {ESC}[7mAVAILABLE PACKAGES{ESC}[m ═══════════╗
{ESC}[3;1H ║
║ {ESC}[4;12H{ESC}[7mA{ESC}[m Program 01
║ {ESC}[5;12H{ESC}[7mB{ESC}[m Program 02
║ {ESC}[6;12H{ESC}[7mC{ESC}[m Program 03
║ {ESC}[7;12H{ESC}[7mD{ESC}[m Program 04
║ {ESC}[8;12H{ESC}[7mE{ESC}[m Program 05
║ {ESC}[9;12H{ESC}[7mF{ESC}[m Program 06
║ {ESC}[10;12H{ESC}[7mG{ESC}[m Program 07
║ {ESC}[11;12H{ESC}[7mH{ESC}[m Program 08
║ {ESC}[12;12H{ESC}[7mI{ESC}[m Program 09
║ {ESC}[4;34H{ESC}[7mJ{ESC}[m Program 10
║ {ESC}[5;34H{ESC}[7mK{ESC}[m Program 11
║ {ESC}[6;34H{ESC}[7mL{ESC}[m Program 12
║ {ESC}[7;34H{ESC}[7mM{ESC}[m Program 13
║ {ESC}[8;34H{ESC}[7mN{ESC}[m Program 14
║ {ESC}[9;34H{ESC}[7mO{ESC}[m Program 15
║ {ESC}[10;34H{ESC}[7mP{ESC}[m Program 16
║ {ESC}[11;34H{ESC}[7mQ{ESC}[m Program 17
║ {ESC}[12;34H{ESC}[7mR{ESC}[m Program 18
║ {ESC}[4;56H{ESC}[7mS{ESC}[m Program 19
║ {ESC}[5;56H{ESC}[7mT{ESC}[m Program 20
║ {ESC}[6;56H{ESC}[7mU{ESC}[m Program 21
║ {ESC}[7;56H{ESC}[7mV{ESC}[m Program 22
║ {ESC}[8;56H{ESC}[7mW{ESC}[m Program 23
║ {ESC}[9;56H{ESC}[7mX{ESC}[m Program 24
║ {ESC}[10;56H{ESC}[7mY{ESC}[m Program 25
║ {ESC}[11;56H{ESC}[7mZ{ESC}[m Program 26
║ {ESC}[12;56H{ESC}[7m@{ESC}[m Ret to DOS
{ESC}[4;79H ║
{ESC}[5;79H ║
{ESC}[6;79H ║
{ESC}[7;79H ║
{ESC}[8;79H ║
{ESC}[9;79H ║
{ESC}[10;79H ║
{ESC}[11;79H ║
{ESC}[12;79H ║
{ESC}[13;1H ╚═══════ {ESC}[7mTYPE A CHARACTER{ESC}[m ═══════╝
{ESC}[m
```

When you have finished entering the information into **Edit** or
Edlin, save your creation under the filename **screen2** then test
it by typing

type screen2

which should cause the following menu to appear on the screen.

```
╔═══════════════════════ AVAILABLE PACKAGES ═══════════════════════╗
║                                                                  ║
║    A Program 01        J Program 10        S Program 19          ║
║    B Program 02        K Program 11        T Program 20          ║
║    C Program 03        L Program 12        U Program 21          ║
║    D Program 04        M Program 13        V Program 22          ║
║    E Program 05        N Program 14        W Program 23          ║
║    F Program 06        O Program 15        X Program 24          ║
║    G Program 07        P Program 16        Y Program 25          ║
║    H Program 08        Q Program 17        Z Program 26          ║
║    I Program 09        R Program 18        @ Ret to DOS          ║
║                                                                  ║
╚═══════════════════════ TYPE A CHARACTER ═════════════════════════╝
```

This menu screen needs to be controlled by an appropriate batch file which we can create using either **Edit** or **Edlin**. Call this batch file **menu5.bat** and include in it the following commands:

```
@echo off
:AGAIN
    type screen2
    echo {ESC}[7mCHOOSE{ESC}[m {ESC}[5m_{ESC}[m
    cursoff
:GETKEY
    respond
    if errorlevel 91 goto GETKEY
    if not errorlevel 64 goto GETKEY
    if errorlevel 64 if not errorlevel 65 goto
QUIT
    echo You have requested a package
    pause
    goto AGAIN
:QUIT
    curson
    cls
```

Note the line with the {ESC} code sequence within the above batch file. It displays the word **CHOOSE** in inverse video and then imitates the presence of a cursor by flashing the underscore character right next to it.

74

Also, note that the **if** commands within the batch file are tested against capital letters codes only. In other words, the input to the file is case sensitive. You will only get the message

```
You have requested a package
Press any key when ready . . .
```

if you choose uppercase letters. The program does not respond to lower case letters or any other keyboard characters. To return to DOS type the key marked '@'.

Being Security Conscious

You can use the information given so far, to obtain some modest security for your system. For example, if you work in an environment where you often need to walk away from your computer for lengthy periods of time and want to keep prying eyes away from your work, then could devise a simple batch file to give you that security without having to switch off your computer. In any case, your computer will last much longer if you avoid switching it on and off too many times during a working day.

Again, use either **Edit** or **Edlin** to write a batch file (call it **sleep.bat**), with the following contents:

```
@echo off
cls
   cursoff
:GETKEY
   respond
   if errorlevel 114 goto GETKEY
   if not errorlevel 113 goto GETKEY
curson
```

Once the **sleep.bat** file is activated, you can only reawaken your computer by typing **q** or Alt+**F10**. You could, of course, choose your own key combination from Table 3.

However, the **sleep.bat** file could be interrupted by pressing repeatedly fast the Ctrl+C or Ctrl+Break keys. Pressing a single Ctrl+C or Ctrl+Break, will have no effect because of the way the **respond.com** file was written, in the first place, with function 07 of interrupt 21, which does not check for Ctrl+Break. But, if while one Ctrl+Break is being processed, another one is issued fairly rapidly behind the first, then the batch file would most likely be interrupted.

Suspending Ctrl+Break:

To overcome the above limitation, two assembly language programs will be created which we will call **brkoff.com** and **brkon.com**, for break-off and break-on, respectively. The DOS service interrupt 21 with function 33 will be used to determine the current status of the operating system's Ctrl+C or Ctrl+Break checking flag. When fetching the status of this flag we let AL=00, while when setting the status of the flag, we let AL=01. Now use either **Edit** or **Edlin** to first create the script file for the break-off situation, with the following contents:

```
a  0100
   mov AH,33
   mov AL,01
   mov DL,00
   int 21
   int 20

r cx
0A
n brkoff.com
w
q
```

then to create the script file for the break-on situation, with the following contents:

```
a  0100
   mov AH,33
   mov AL,01
   mov DL,01
   int 21
   int 20

r cx
0A
n brkon.com
w
q
```

Finally, use **Debug** successively with redirection, first to the break-off script file, then to the break-on script file, to produce the two programs **brkoff.com** and **brkon.com**.

Now create the controlling batch file (call it **secure.bat**), with the following contents:

```
@echo off
 cls
   cursoff
   brkoff
:GETKEY
   respond
   if errorlevel 114 goto GETKEY
   if not errorlevel 113 goto GETKEY
curson
brkon
```

When **secure.bat** is activated, Ctr+Break has no effect and cannot be used to terminate the batch file.

By also inserting the command **secure** in an appropriate place within the **autoexec.bat** file, it is possible to make your system even more secure. Its position would depend on whether or not the actual batch file **secure.bat** and all the .COM programs it uses are to be found in the root directory or not. If not, then the command **secure** must be inserted after the PATH declaration in which case it is possible to use Ctrl+Break early enough to terminate the **autoexec.bat** file before the **secure** command is reached.

7. COMMAND SUMMARY

The following is a summary of the commands supported by the MS-DOS operating environment. For a fuller explanation of both commands and options, consult your system's PC/MS-DOS reference manual. The various commands are labelled internal or external, with external commands being accessible to the user only if the full filespec (drive and path) is given to where the appropriate command file resides.

Command	Explanation
append	External - sets a path that MS-DOS will search for data files when they are not in the current directory. It can even be told not to search already defined paths.

Example: append c:\wproc\docs

searches the \wproc\docs directory on drive c: for data files.

assign	External - assigns a drive letter to a different drive.

Example: assign a=c

allows all references to drive a: to go to the c: drive.

attrib [filespec]	External - sets or resets the *read only* attribute & archive bit of a file, and displays the attributes of a file.

Switches:

+r   sets read-only mode of a file
–r   disables read-only mode
+a   sets the archive bit of a file
–a   clears the archive bit.

Example: attrib +R filespec

backup [filespec]   External - backs up one or more files from one disc to another. It can also automatically format the destination disc.

Switches:

/a   adds files to be backed up to those already on the backup disc without erasing old files

/d   backs up only those files which were modified after that date

/l   makes a backup log entry in a file called BACKUP.LOG.

/f:*size*

causes the target disc to be formatted to a size which is different from the default size of the disc drive. Use one of the following values for size, which specifies the capacity of the disc in Kbytes:

160 / 180 for single-sided, double-density 5¼" discs,
320 / 360 for double-sided, double-density 5¼" discs,
720 for double-sided, double-density 3½" discs,
1200 for double-sided, high-capacity 5¼" discs,
1440 for double-sided, high-capacity 3½" discs,
2880 for 2.88 MB, double-sided, 3½" discs.

/m   includes files that have been changed since last backup

/s   backs up sub-directory files to file in current directory

/t:*time*
> to back-up only files modified at or after the specified time

/L:*filename*
> to create a log file, called *filename*, in which is stored a record of the current BACKUP operation.

Example: backup c:\ a:/s

backs up all files on the c: drive onto the a: drive.

break	Internal - sets the Ctrl+Break or the Ctrl+C switch.

Example: break ON

cd (or chdir)	Internal - changes the working directory to a different directory.

Example: cd\wproc\docs

chcp [nnn]	Internal - selects current code page for as many devices as possible. Omitting *nnn* displays the current code page.

chkdsk [filespec]	External - analyses the directories, files, and File Allocation Table on the logged or designated drive and produces a status report. It also reports the volume, serial number and disc allocation units.

Switches:

/f   fixes any problems found during the check

/v   causes the display of filespecs as they are being processed.

Example: chkdsk a:/f/v

cls	Internal - clears the screen.

command [filespec] External - starts the command processor which is loaded into memory in two parts; the resident part and the transient part. If the transient part is overwritten by a program, it is reloaded.

Switches:

/e specifies the environment size in bytes (default = 160 bytes)

/p prohibits command.com from exiting to a higher level

/c executes a following command

Example: command /c chkdsk a:

starts a new command processor under the current program, runs the chkdsk command on the disc in the A: drive, and returns to the first command processor.

comp External - compares two files and reports any differences.

Switches:

/a displays differences as characters

/c performs a comparison that is not case-sensitive

/d displays differences in decimal format

/l displays the number of the line on which differences occur

/n= compares the first specified number of lines of both files.

Example: comp file1 file2

copy [filespec]	Internal - copies one or more files to specified disc. If preferred, copies can be given different names. Switches: /a indicates an ASCII text file /b indicates a binary file /v causes the verification of data written on the destination disc. Example: copy *.exe a:/v copies all files with the .exe extension to the a: drive with verification.
ctty	Internal - changes the standard I/O console to an auxiliary (aux) console, and vice versa. Example: ctty aux moves all input/output from the current device (console) to an aux port such as another terminal. The command *ctty con* moves I/O back to the console.
date	Internal - enters or changes the current date.
debug	External - starts the debug program that allows you to create or edit executable files.
del [filespec]	Internal - deletes all files with the designated filespec. Switch: /p displays filenames to confirm deletion. Example: del a:*.txt deletes all .txt files from the a: drive.

dir [filespec]	Internal - lists the files in a directory.

Switches:

/p   displays the directory listing a page at a time

/w   displays the directory listing in wide format

/s   lists every occurrence, in the specified directory and all subdirectories, of the specified filename

/o: controls the sort order in which a directory listing is displayed. For example,

     n   in alphabetical order

     –n   in reverse alphabetical order

     e   in alphabetical order by extension

     –e   in reverse alphabetical order by extension

     d   by date & time, earliest first

     –d   by date & time, latest first

     s   by size, smallest first

     –s   by size, largest first

     g   with directories grouped before files

     –g   with directories grouped after files.

diskcomp	External - compares the contents of the disc in the source drive to the disc in the destination drive.

diskcopy	External - copies the contents of the disc in the source drive to the disc in the destination drive.

Switch:

/v   verifies correct copying.

doskey	External - starts the doskey program which recalls MS-DOS commands.

Switches:

/history   displays a list of all commands stored in memory. The switch can be used with the re-direction symbol (>) to redirect the list to a file

/macros   displays a list of all doskey macros. The switch can be used with the re-direction symbol (>) to redirect the list to a file

/bufsize=   allows the specification of the buffer size to be used for storing commands. The default size is 512 bytes, while the minimum buffer size is 256 bytes.

dosshell	External - activates the front-end graphical interface.

edit	External - activates the MS-DOS screen editor which is used to create or edit ASCII text files.

Switches:

/b   displays the editor in black and white

/g   uses the fastest screen updating for CGA displays

/h   displays the maximum number of lines possible for the monitor you are using.

edlin	External - activates the line editor edlin which can be used to create and edit ASCII text files.
EMM386	External - enables or disables expanded memory support on a computer with an 80386 or higher processor.
exe2bin	External - converts .exe files to binary format.
exit	Internal - exits the command processor and returns to a previous level.
expand	External - expands a compressed MS-DOS version 5 file.
fastopen [filespec]	External - store in memory the location of directories and recently opened files on a specified drive.

fastopen [filespec] Switch:

/x   allows use of expanded memory. If this switch is used, then the /x switch must also be used with the **buffers** command.

fc [filespec]   External - compares two files and displays the differences between them.

Switches:

/a   abbreviates the output of an ASCII comparison to only the first and last line of each set of differences
/b   compares binary files
/c   ignores the case of letters

/l	compares ASCII files line by line
/n	displays the line numbers during an ASCII comparison
/t	does not expand tabs to spaces
/w	compresses tabs and spaces during the comparison.

fdisk External - sets up and partitions the fixed disc for use with MS-DOS and other operating systems. This command is also used to display and change the current active partition. It also supports an 80-column screen. It also has improved user-friendly commands to allow disc partitioning in megabytes or percentages instead of cylinders.

fdiskoff External - could have another name, but its use is to park the fixed disc heads. This should be done before moving a computer equipped with a hard disc to prevent disc damage.

find [filespec] External - searches for a specific string of text in a specified ASCII file or files.

Switches:

/v	displays all lines not containing the specified string
/c	prints the count of lines containing the string
/n	precedes each occurrence with the relative line number in the file
/i	search is insensitive to the case of letters.

Example: find "lost words" chap1

searches for the string *lost words* (which must appear within full quotes) in the named file (chap1).

format [filespec]

External - formats the disc in the specified drive.

Switches:

/8   formats with 8 sectors per track

/4   formats a double-sided disc with 40 tracks, 9 sectors per track for 360 KB in a high capacity (1.2 MB) disc drive per track

/n   specifies the number of sectors per track, i.e. /n:9 for nine sectors

/t   specifies the number of tracks, i.e. /t:40 for forty tracks

/s   copies the system files from the logged drive

/q   deletes the file allocation table (FAT) and the root directory of a previously formatted disc

/f:*size*

specifies the size of the disc to be formatted. Use one of the following values for size, which specifies the capacity of the disc in Kbytes:

160 / 180 for single-sided, double-density 5¼" discs,

320 / 360 for double-sided, double-density 5¼" discs,

720 for double-sided, double-density 3½" discs,

1200 for double-sided, high-capacity 5¼" discs,

1440 for double-sided, high-capacity
3½" discs,
2880 for 2.88 MB, double-sided, 3½"
discs.

/v   allows a volume label to be
given to the disc after the for-
matting process

/v:label
allows you to specify *label*
without prompting after the for-
matting process

Example: format a:/4/s

graftabl   External - loads a custom designed,
colour graphics font table into mem-
ory. It also supports the multilingual
code page 850.

Switch:

/status
identifies the code page selected for use by graftabl.

graphics   External - it supports EGA and VGA
graphics modes to provide screen
dumps to IBM Graphics, Proprinters
and compatibles.

Switches:

/r   prints the image as it appears
on the screen (white characters on a black background,
rather than reversed)

/b   prints the background in colour

/lcd prints an image by using the
liquid crystal display aspect
ratio instead of the CGA aspect ratio.

help	External - provides online information about the MS-DOS commands.
install	External - it provides an improved method of loading memory-resident pop-up programs.
join	External - joins a disc drive to a specific path.

Switch:

/d   cancels any previous join commands for the specified drive.

keyb [xx]	External - selects a special keyboard layout. Omitting **xx** returns the current status of the keyboard.

Switches:

/e   specifies that an enhanced keyboard is installed
/id: specifies the keyboard in use.

label	External - creates or changes the volume identification label on a disc.
loadhigh (lh)	Internal - loads a program into the upper memory area.
md (or mkdir)	Internal - creates a new directory on the specified disc.
mem	External - it reports the amounts of conventional, expanded and extended memory that are available.

Switches:

/c   displays the status of programs loaded in conventional and upper memory area

	/d displays the status of currently loaded programs and of internal drivers
	/p displays the status of programs that are currently loaded into memory.
mirror	External - activates the mirror program which records information about one or more discs. The unformat and undelete commands use this information.

mirror — continued:

Switches:

/l   retains only the latest information about the disc.

/t:drive
   loads a TSR (terminate-and-stay-resident) program that records information used by the undelete command to recover deleted files.

mode [options]   External - sets the mode of operation on a display monitor, parallel/serial printer or the RS232C port. The keyboard repetition and auto-repeat start delay time can be set. Also, it allows the setting of the number of rows to any of 25, 43 or 50 on the screen, and there is a wider range of serial-port configurations.

Options:

Display: mode [n]

40   sets display width to 40 characters per line

80   sets display width to 80 characters per line

bw40	sets screen to black and white display with 40 characters
bw80	sets screen to black and white display with 80 characters
co40	sets screen to colour display with 40 characters
co80	sets screen to colour display with 80 characters
mono	sets screen to monochrome with 80 characters.

Printer: mode LPTi: [n][,[m][,p]]

i	sets printer number with legal values from 1 to 3
n	sets number of characters per line with legal values of 80 or 132
m	sets the number of lines per inch with legal values of 6 or 8
p	allows continuous re-entry on a time-out error.

Example: mode LPT1: 132,8

sets the printer in the first parallel port to 132 characters per line and 8 lines per inch.

Serial printer: mode LPTi: = COMj
This command redirects all output sent to one of the parallel printer ports to one of the serial (RS232C) ports. Before using this command, the serial port must be initialized using the *p* switch of the printer mode command.

i	sets printer number with legal values from 1 to 3

	j	sets the serial port with legal values of 1 or 2.

more External - sends output to the console one screen-full at a time.

Example: type read.me | more

displays the contents of the read.me file one screen at a time.

nlsfunc External - provides support for extended country information and allows the use of **chcp** command to select code pages for all devices defined as having code page switching support.

path Internal - sets and displays the path to be searched by DOS for external commands or batch files.

Example: path c:\;c:\dos;c:\comms

will search the root directory as well as the dos and comms sub-directories for files with .COM, .EXE, and .BAT extensions.

print [filespec] External - can be used to print text files in background mode, while other tasks are being performed. Using the command without options displays files already in the print queue.

Switches:

/d   specifies the print device such as PRN or AUX

/b   sets size of internal buffer with legal values from 512 to 16384 bytes, speeding up printing

/q	specifies the number of files in the print queue, normally 10, with legal values from 4 to 32
/t	allows cancellation of files in print queue
/c	allows cancellation of files in the print queue. It can be used with the /p switch
/p	allows the addition of files to the print queue. Both /c & /p can be used in the same command line.

prompt   Internal - changes the command prompt.

Example: pg

which allows the path of the current working directory to be displayed as the prompt.

qbasic   External - activates the MS-DOS QBasic program that reads instructions written in the Basic computer language.

Switches:

/b	displays QBasic in black and white
/g	provides the fastest update of a CGA monitor
/h	displays the maximum number of display lines possible for the type of monitor used
/editor	activates the MS-DOS screen editor
/run	runs the specified Basic program before displaying it.

rd (or rmdir)	Internal - removes the specified directory.
recover	External - recovers a file or an entire disc containing bad sectors.
ren (or rename)	Internal - changes the file name.

Example: ren a:\docs\mem1 mem2

will rename the mem1 file, which is to be found in sub-directory docs on a disc in the a: drive, to mem2.

replace [filespec]	External - allows easy updating of files from a source disc to a target disc of files having the same name.

Switches:

/a   adds new files that exist on the source disc but not on the target disc. You can not use this switch with the /s or /u switch

/p   prompts the user before replacing

/r   replaces read only files, as well as unprotected files

/s   searches all subdirectories of the destination directory and replaces matching files. You can not use the /s switch with the /a switch

/u   updates files with a time and date on the source disc more recent than those on the destination disc. You can not use the /u switch with the /a switch

/w   waits for you to insert a disc before replace begins to search for source files.

restore [filespec]	External - restores one or more files that were backed up using the *backup* command.

Switches:

/s restores files in the specified directory and all files in any sub-directories of the specified directory

/p prompts user before overwriting an existing file by restoring

/a:date restores only those files last modified on or after the specified date. The date format varies according to the country setting in the CONFIG.SYS file

/b:date restores only those files last modified on or before the specified date.

/e:time restores only those files last modified on or before the specified time. The time format varies according to the country setting in the CONFIG.SYS file

/l:time restores only those files last modified on or after the specified time.

/m restores only those files modified since the last backup

/u restores only those files that no longer exist on the destination disc

/d displays a list of the files on the backup disc that match the names specified in *filename* without restoring any files.

set	Internal - sets strings into the command processor's environment. The general form of the command is:

set [name=[parameter]]

Set by itself displays the current environment.

setver	External - sets the MS-DOS version number that version 5 reports to a program.

share	External - installs file sharing and locking.

Switches:

/f: allocates file space, in bytes. The default value is 2048
/l: sets the number of files that can be locked at one time. The default is 20.

sort [filespec]	External - reads data from the console or a file, sorts it and sends it to the console or file.

Switches:

/r   sorts in reverse order
/+n   sorts the file according to the character in column n.

Example: dir | sort

sorts the output of the *dir* command in alphabetical order.

subst	External - allows substitution of a virtual drive for an existing drive and path.

Switch:

/d   deletes a virtual drive.

Example: subst d: a:\wproc\docs

will cause future reference to drive d: to be taken as replacement to the longer reference to a:\wproc\docs.

switches
External - it forces the conventional keyboard layout on to an enhanced keyboard.

sys
External - transfers the PC/MS-DOS system files from the logged drive to the disc in the specified drive. It also allows the specification of source drive and path commands to transfer system files across a network.

time
Internal - displays and sets the system time. It also supports a 12- or 24-hour format.

tree
External - displays the directory structure in graphical form.

Switches:

/f   displays the names of the files in each directory

/a   specifies that tree is to use text characters instead of graphic characters.

type
Internal - displays the contents of a file on the console.

undelete
External - restores files which were previously deleted with the del command.

Switches:

/list   lists deleted files that are available to be recovered

	/all recovers all deleted files without prompting
	/dos recovers only those files that are internally listed as deleted by MS-DOS, prompting for confirmation
	/dt recovers only the files listed in the delection-tracking file produced by the mirror command.
unformat	External - restores a disc erased by the format command or restructured by the recover command.

Switches:

/j	verifies that the file created by the mirror command has been saved and that it agrees with the listed information on the disc
/u	unformats a disc without using the mirror file
/l	when used with the /partn switch, lists every file and subdirectory found by unformat
/p	sends output messages to the printer connected to LPT1
/test	shows how unformat will recreate the information of the disc
/partn	
	restores a corrupted partition table of a hard disc drive.

ver	Internal - displays the PC/MS-DOS version number.
verify	Internal - allows the verify switch to be turned ON or OFF.

Example: verify OFF

99

vol	Internal - displays the disc volume label, if it exists.
xcopy [filespec]	External - copies files and directories, including lower level sub-directories, if they exist, to the destination drive and directory.

Switches:

/a   copies source files that have their archive bit set

/d: copies source files which were modified on or after a specified date

/e   copies sub-directories even if they are empty - use this switch in conjunction with /s

/m   copies archived files only, but also turns off the archive bit in the source file

/p   prompts the user with '(Y/N?)'

/s   copies directories and their sub-directories unless they are empty

/v   causes verification of each file as it is written

/w   displays a message before starting to copy.

APPENDIX A

THE MS-DOS EDITOR

MS-DOS provides you with a full screen editor, called **Edit**, with which you can create special ASCII files that customise your system. These are text files which, when sent to the screen or printer, are interpreted as text, unlike the .COM or .EXE files which are binary files. **Edit** can also be used to create the source code of programming languages, such as Fortran and C. In such cases, do remember to give the files the appropriate extension (**.for** and **.c**, for the above two, respectively).

To invoke **Edit**, the MS-DOS system start-up disc or a disc that contains it, must be accessible and the full path of the file you want to create or edit must be specified. Thus, typing

```
C:\>edit test.txt
```

expects to find both **Edit** and the fictitious file **test.txt** on the disc in the logged drive (in this case C:), while typing

```
C:\>edit A:test.txt
```

expects to find **Edit** on the C: drive, and the file **test.txt** on the disc in the A: drive.

If the file does not exist on the specified disc or directory, then **Edit** displays a blank screen, as follows:

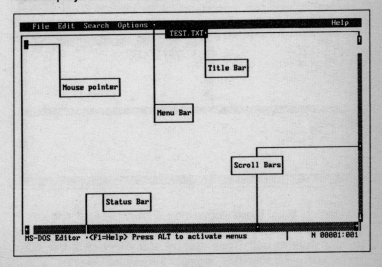

The **Edit** screen is subdivided into several areas which have the following function:

Area	*Function*
Menu bar	allows you to choose from several main menu options
Title bar	displays the name of the current file. If a new file, it displays the word <Untitled>
Status bar	displays the current file status and information regarding the present process
Scroll bar	allows you to scroll the screen with the use of the mouse.

The area bounded by the Title bar and the two Scroll bars is known as the view window. It is in this area that you enter the contents of a new file or load and view the contents of an old file.

The **Edit** screen can also be invoked from within DOS Shell by selecting the **Editor** from the Main group of programs, as shown below:

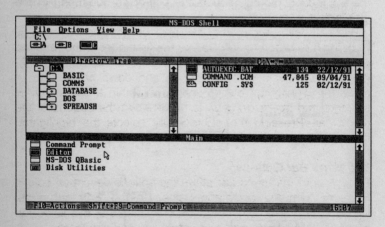

On starting **Edit**, the dialogue box shown overleaf appears in the middle of the screen asking you to type in the name of the file you want to edit. Type **test.txt** and either click the <OK> button in the dialogue box, or press the <Enter> key.

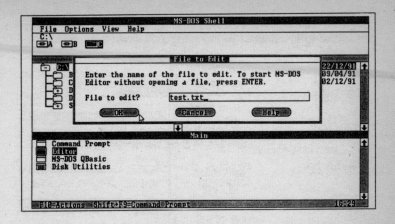

The Editor Menu Bar

Each menu bar option on the editor, has associated with it a pull-down sub-menu. To activate the menu bar, either press the <Alt> key, which causes the first item on the menu bar (in this case File) to be highlighted, then use the right and left arrow keys to highlight any of the items of the menu bar, or use the mouse to point to an item. Pressing either the <Enter> key, or the left mouse button, reveals the pull-down sub-menu of the highlighted menu item.

The pull-down sub-menus can also be activated directly by pressing the <Alt> key followed by the first letter of the required menu option. Thus pressing **Alt+O**, causes the Options sub-menu to be displayed. Use the up and down arrow keys to move the highlighted bar up and down within a sub-menu, or the right and left arrow keys to move along the options of the menu bar. Pressing the <Enter> key selects the highlighted option, while pressing the <Esc> key closes the menu system.

The Menu Bar Options:

Each item of the menu bar offers the options described below. However, dimmed command names in the **Edit** sub-menu indicate that these commands are unavailable at this time; you might need to select some text before you can use them.

The information given below can be displayed by highlighting the required sub-menu option and pressing the **F1** help key. This same information is listed overleaf for easier reference.

The File Sub-Menu

Selecting **File** causes the following pull-down sub-menu to be displayed:

New: Use to create a new document file.

Open: Use to open an existing document so you can edit or print it.

Save: Use to save the current version of your document.

Save As: Use to save your document as a file.

To preserve the previous version of your document, rename it in the File Name dialogue box.

Print: Use to print all or part of a document.

Exit: Use to quit the MS-DOS Editor environment.

The Edit Sub-Menu

Selecting **Edit** causes the following pull-down sub-menu to be displayed:

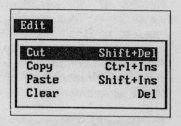

Cut: Use to remove selected text and put it on the Clipboard, a temporary holding area.

Copy: Use to copy selected text to the Clipboard. The original text remains unchanged.

Paste: Use to insert a block of text from the Clipboard at any point in a document.

Clear: Use to delete selected text without copying it to the Clipboard. The Clipboard's contents remain unchanged.

The Search Sub-Menu

Selecting **Search** causes the following pull-down sub-menu to be displayed:

Find: Use to search for a text string. You can request a case-sensitive match or a whole-word match.

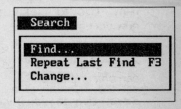

Repeat Last Find: Use to repeat the search performed by the most recent Find or Change command.

Change: Use to replace one text string with another.

The Options Sub-Menu

Selecting **Options** causes the following pull-down sub-menu to be displayed:

Display: Use to control screen colour, scroll bars in windows, and the number of spaces the <Tab> key advances the cursor.

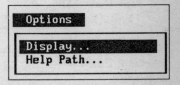

Help Path: Use to change the directories that the MS-DOS Editor searches to find the Help file EDIT.HLP

Help Menu

Selecting **Help** causes the following pull-down sub-menu to be displayed:

Getting Started: Use to find out about using MS-DOS Editor menus, commands, and dialogue boxes. Also to get Help on using the Editor and using options when starting the Editor.

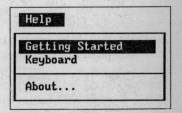

Keyboard: Use to find out about keystrokes for performing tasks on the MS-DOS Editor, and the WordStar keystrokes that can be used with the Editor.

About: Use to display the version number and copyright information for the MS-DOS Editor.

Dialogue Boxes:

Three periods after a sub-menu option, means that a dialogue box will open when the option is selected. A dialogue box is used for the insertion of additional information, such as the name of a file to be opened, or to be acted upon in some way.

To understand dialogue boxes, type the word 'hi' in the edit screen, then press **Alt+S**, and select the **Change** option from the revealed sub-menu of **Search**. The dialogue box shown below will now appear on the screen.

```
┌─────────────────────── Change ───────────────────────┐
│                                                       │
│  Find What: ┌───────────────────────────────────────┐ │
│             │ hi                                     │ │
│             └───────────────────────────────────────┘ │
│                                                       │
│  Change To: ┌───────────────────────────────────────┐ │
│             │ hello                                  │ │
│             └───────────────────────────────────────┘ │
│                                                       │
│                                                       │
│      [ ] Match Upper/Lowercase        [ ] Whole Word  │
│                                                       │
│  ◄ Find and Verify ► < Change All > < Cancel > < Help > │
│                                                       │
└───────────────────────────────────────────────────────┘
```

The <Tab> key can be used to move the cursor from one field to another within a dialogue box, while the <Enter> key is only used to indicate that the options within the various fields within the dialogue box are specified correctly. Every dialogue box contains one field which is enclosed in emboldened angle-brackets (<Find and Verify>, in the above example). This field indicates the action that **Edit** will take if the <Enter> key is pressed (in our example, the word 'hi' will be changed to 'hello', if this is what we choose to type against the 'Find What' and 'Change To' fields. Pressing the <Esc> key aborts the menu option and returns you to the editor.

106

The cursor can be moved to any part of the text being typed in the view window, and corrections can be made, with the use of the key strokes described below.

Key	Function
Left Arrow	moves the cursor to the left by one character
Right Arrow	moves the cursor to the right by one character
Ctrl+Left Arrow	moves the cursor to the beginning of the previous word on the current line
Ctrl+Right Arrow	moves the cursor to the beginning of the next word on the current line
Home	moves the cursor to the first column of the current line
End	moves the cursor to the end of the last word on the current line
Up Arrow	moves the cursor up one line
Down Arrow	moves the cursor down one line
Ctrl+Home	moves the cursor to the first line of the current screen
Ctrl+End	moves the cursor to the last line of the current screen
PgUp	moves the cursor to the previous screen
PgDn	moves the cursor to the next screen
Ctrl+PgUp	moves the cursor left one screen
Ctrl+PgDn	moves the cursor right one screen
Ins	toggles the Insert mode from ON (its default position) to OFF and back again
Enter	moves the cursor to the beginning of the next line, provided the insert mode is in the ON position
Ctrl+Y	deletes the line at the current cursor position
Ctrl+N	inserts a blank line at the current cursor position
Shift+Arrows	marks block areas on the screen to be used with the sub-menu of the Edit option, namely Cut, Copy, Paste, and Clear.

When areas of text are marked, with either the use of the **Shift+Arrows** or by clicking and dragging the mouse, **Edit** keeps the contents of the blocked (highlighted) area of text in a temporary storage area known as the 'Clipboard' from which it can be retrieved later when the **Cut**, **Copy**, and **Paste** options are used. The Clipboard stores only one block of information at a time. If you attempt to store a second block of information, it simply overrides the previously stored block.

If you are not using a mouse, you might want to clear the scroll bars from the screen, to give you more room. This can be done by pressing **Alt+O**, selecting the **Display** option and pressing the <Tab> key until the cursor is positioned in the 'Scroll Bars' field. Pressing the spacebar toggles the option into the off position by clearing the letter X from within the square brackets.

If you are using a mouse, scrolling text in the view window is easy. Place the mouse pointer on the top, bottom, left or right of the scroll bars and click the left mouse button to scroll upwards, downwards, to the left or to the right, respectively.

There are a lot more commands associated with **Edit**, but you'll find that the ones given above are sufficient for almost all your needs.

Creating & Saving a Text File
As an example, type the following four lines in **Edit**'s view window:

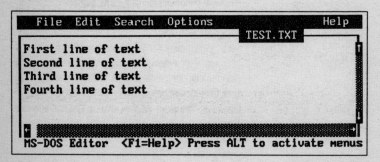

Editing Text:
To edit any part of the document, use the up or down arrow keys to place the cursor at the beginning of the line you want to

edit, then use the right or left arrow keys to place the cursor at the required position where you want to begin editing.

If you have a mouse, simply point to the place you want to edit and click the left mouse button to place the cursor at the position occupied by the mouse pointer.

Use one of the above techniques to change the second line of our document to

```
Second line of text, edited
```

Selecting Text:
To select text, place the cursor at the required starting position, and while holding down the <Shift> key, press the right or left arrow keys to highlight as much of the text on that line as you like. With the mouse, place the mouse pointer at the required starting position and while holding down the left mouse button, move the mouse horizontally to the right or left to highlight the required text on that line.

If you try to select text which runs to more than one line, the whole line (first and subsequent) will be selected. Thus, you can either select text from part of a line, or you select text from whole lines.

As an example, select the words ' of text' (including the leading space) from the second line, as shown below:

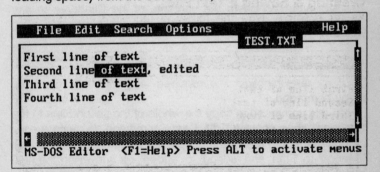

Moving Text:
Having selected the part of text you want to move, use the **Edit, Cut** command, then place the cursor at the required point where you would like to move the text to, and use the **Edit, Paste** command.

As an example, select the words ' of text' (including the leading space) from the second line, then use the **Edit, Cut**, followed by the **Edit, Paste** commands, to move the selected text to the end of the fourth line. The result is shown below:

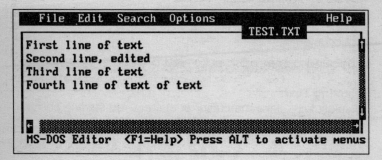

```
    File  Edit  Search  Options              Help
                                   TEST.TXT
  First line of text
  Second line, edited
  Third line of text
  Fourth line of text of text


 MS-DOS Editor  <F1=Help> Press ALT to activate menus
```

Clearing Text:

To remove text from a document without changing the contents of the Clipboard, highlight the unwanted text, then use the **Edit, Clear** command.

Use this command to remove from the fourth line both repetitions of the words 'of text', then, to prove that the contents of the Clipboard have not changed, use the **Edit, Paste** command to restore the fourth line to its original form.

In fact, you can paste the contents of the Clipboard to any part of a document, as many times as you like, because pasting does not empty the Clipboard.

Copying Text:

To copy text, highlight the required text, then use the **Edit, Copy** command.

Use this command to copy the whole of the second line to the Clipboard, then use the **Edit, Paste** command, to paste a copy of it on to the fifth line of the document. Next, change the words 'Second' to 'Fifth' and 'edited' to 'added', as shown on the next page.

You will have to use the <Del> key to delete the unwanted words as the editor is normally in 'insert' mode and when typing text it inserts it at the cursor position. To toggle the edit mode from 'insert' to 'overtype', press the <Ins> key once.

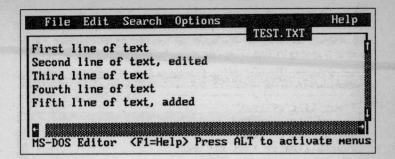

```
 File  Edit  Search  Options                        Help
                              TEST.TXT
First line of text
Second line of text, edited
Third line of text
Fourth line of text
Fifth line of text, added

MS-DOS Editor   <F1=Help> Press ALT to activate menus
```

Finding Text:

To find a specific word or part of a word, use the **Search, Find**
command which causes the following dialogue box to appear
on your screen:

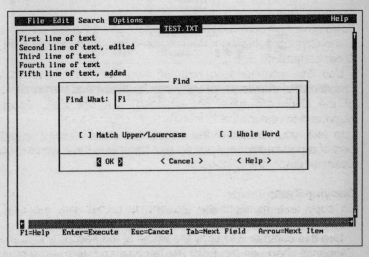

```
 File  Edit  Search  Options                        Help
                              TEST.TXT
First line of text
Second line of text, edited
Third line of text
Fourth line of text
Fifth line of text, added
        ┌───────────────── Find ─────────────────┐
        │ Find What: │Fi                          │
        │                                         │
        │ [ ] Match Upper/Lowercase   [ ] Whole Word │
        │    ◄ OK ►      < Cancel >     < Help >   │
        └─────────────────────────────────────────┘

 F1=Help   Enter=Execute   Esc=Cancel   Tab=Next Field   Arrow=Next Item
```

Note that the word nearest to the cursor is offered in the 'Find
What' field as a default. In the above example, if the cursor is at
the beginning of the document, the default word will be 'First'.

As an example, to find all the words that begin with the letters
'Fi', after typing these in the 'Find What' field, press the <**OK**>
button. **Edit** highlights the first word containing these letters,
and to find the next occurrence you will have to use the **Search,
Repeat Last Find** command.

Saving a Document:

To save a document that you have already named, use the **File, Save** command. To save an unnamed document, or to save it under a different name, use the **File, Save As** command which causes the following dialogue box to appear on your screen:

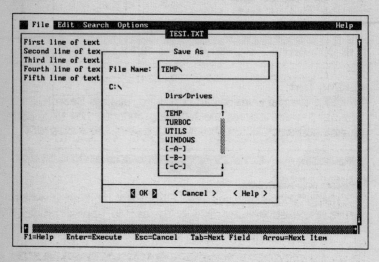

Note that you can save a document to any subdirectory or drive by selecting appropriately from the Dirs/Drives list within the dialogue box.

Opening a Document:

Once a document has been saved to a file on disc, you can open it by using the **File, Open** command which causes the dialogue box shown on the next page to appear on your screen.

Again, you can select any of the **.txt** files (which is the default file extension) from the logged drive and subdirectory, or indeed change the extension to, say, **.bat** if you want to work with batch files such as the **autoexec.bat** file.

Also note that you can change the logged directory or drive by selecting appropriately from the Dirs/Drives list within the dialogue box.

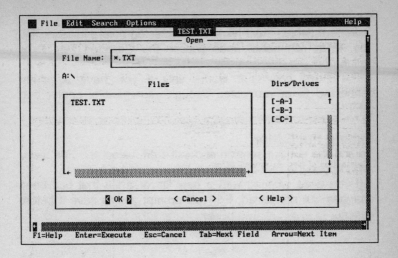

Printing a Document:

To print a document, use the **File, Print** command which causes the dialogue box, shown below, to appear on your screen:

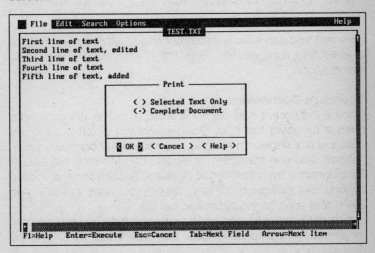

Note that you can choose to print the complete document (which is the default setting), or a pre-selected part of the document. If you are printing the whole document, simply press the <OK> button, but if you are printing a selected part of the document (which must have been selected before initiating the **File, Print** command), then choose the 'Selected Text Only' option from the dialogue box.

The **Print** command works only if you have a printer connected to or redirected through your parallel printer port (LPT1).

Exiting the Editor

To end the current session and exit **Edit**, select the **File** menu and choose the **Exit** option from the revealed sub-menu.

If you were working with a new file or a file that had been changed but not saved, **Edit** will prompt you to save it before exiting.

APPENDIX B

THE EDLIN LINE EDITOR

MS-DOS provides you with a simple line editor, called EDLIN, and you should become familiar with its use. In general, **Edlin** allows the creation and editing of ASCII files. These are text files which when sent to the screen or printer are interpreted as text, unlike the .COM or .EXE files which are binary.

Edlin can also be used to create the source code of various programming languages, such as Fortran and C. In such cases, remember to give the file the appropriate extension, which for the two languages mentioned, are **.for** and **.c**, respectively. However, if you intend to write large programs which might require extensive editing, you might be better off using a full screen editor or your word processor, provided it can save files in ASCII format.

To invoke **Edlin**, the MS-DOS System disc or a disc that contains it must be in one drive, and the file you want to create or edit must be specified. Thus, typing the command:

```
C:\>edlin test.txt
```

expects to find both **Edlin** and the fictitious file **test.txt** on the disc in the logged drive (in this case C:), while typing

```
C:\>edlin A:test.txt
```

expects to find **Edlin** on the disc in the logged drive and the file **test.txt** on the disc in the A: drive.

If the file does not exist on the specified disc, then **Edlin** responds with

```
New File
*_
```

and waits for further commands, while if the file already exists, then **Edlin** loads the file into RAM and responds with

```
End of input file
*_
```

Note the '*' prompt which is characteristic of **Edlin**.

Creating a Text File

Let us now create a text file, called **test.txt**, which we will use to demonstrate the power of **Edlin**. To start, type at the MS-DOS prompt

```
C:\>edlin test.txt
```

which should cause **Edlin** to respond with

```
New File
*_
```

if that file does not exist on your disc. If it does exist and you do not want to spoil its contents, then type **q** (for quit) and press the <Enter> key.

The Insert Command on a New File:

To insert lines of text, use the command **i** (for insert) at the prompt. In the case of a new file, as no lines of text exist in the file, type 1i and then type in the short text given below.

```
*1i
        1:*first line of text
        2:*second line of text
        3:*^C
*_
```

After typing 1i at the prompt, **Edlin** responds by giving a new line number (in this case 1:) with an asterisk after it to indicate that this is the current line. At this point we type 'first line of text'. On pressing the <Enter> key, **Edlin** gives us an additional line number, now 2:*, into which we type 'second line of text'. Again, on pressing <Enter>, we are offered a further line number, and so on. To end the insertion mode, type Ctrl+C. The character ^C is the two-key depression Ctrl+C.

The List Command:

To see what text is in the file, type **l** (for list) at the prompt, as follows:

```
*l
        1: first line of text
        2:*second line of text
*_
```

116

The line numbers are inserted by **Edlin** so that you can refer to the line you want to edit. The '*' in line 2 indicates that this line was the last to be edited or inserted when **Edlin** was used last. Note that now there is only one current line. Should the file you are listing be very long, listing in this manner causes the current line to appear in the middle of the listing.

To list specific lines, use the **l** command with line numbers. For example,

```
*5,151
```

will list lines from 5 to 15 inclusive. Note the syntax of the command which is: "From line number to line number Command". There must be no comma between the second line number and the command letter.

The Edit Mode
To change the current line, type the new line number and press <Enter>. This puts you in edit mode and will cause the line whose number you typed to be displayed. Pressing <Enter> again, confirms that you are happy with the contents of that line, otherwise you can either press the right cursor key to reveal each letter of that line, or re-type the entire line, making any necessary changes. In our case, we want to change line 2 to

```
second line of text, edited
```

so enter the edit mode and change the line appropriately. This is best done by using the right arrow cursor key to reveal the whole of the existing line and then typing the extra information at the end of it. The <Ins> and <Del> keys can also be used to edit the text.

The Insert Command on an Existing File:
To insert lines of text, use the command **i** (for insert) at the prompt. However, be warned. Using **i** by its own will insert the new line before the current line (the one with the * after the line number). To insert lines at any other point, give the line number before the command.

In our case, we would like to insert two additional lines after the existing two. To do this, type

117

```
*3i
      3:*third line of text
      4:*fourth line of text
      5:*^C
*_
```

Again, insertion mode is terminated in line 5: by pressing Ctrl+C. If we now list the contents of the file, we get:

```
*l
      1: first line of text
      2: second line of text, edited
      3: third line of text
      4:*fourth line of text
*_
```

The last line to be inserted becomes the current line.

The Delete Command:
To delete unwanted lines of text, use the **d** command (for delete) at the prompt. However, if you use the **d** command without any number associated with it, you will delete the current line (the one with the asterisk). Therefore, if you want to delete line 13, say, type

```
*13d
```

or if you want to delete a group of lines, type

```
*13,15d
```

which is translated as 'lines 13 to 15 to be deleted'.

The Move & Copy Commands:
To move or copy text, use the **m** or **c** commands (for move or copy). These commands must be preceded by three numbers, as follows:

```
*13,15,8m
```

which is interpreted as 'lines 13 to 15 to be moved to a position before line 8'.

Similarly, the **c** command will copy a block and insert it before the given line. To move or copy a single line, the first two numbers in the command must be the same. After moving or copying lines, use the list command to force line re-numbering.

The Search Command:

To search for the occurrence of a word or a specified number of characters in a file you have created using **Edlin**, use the search command. Just as in the list and delete commands, a line range is first specified, followed by the **s** (for search) command. Thus, typing

```
*1,4s edited
```

evokes the response

```
        2: second line of text, edited
 *_
```

which displays the line containing the word 'edited'.

Note that the space between the command **s** and the word 'edited' becomes part of the search string. Had we been searching for the characters 'con' within the word 'second', we would have had to omit the space between the command s and the string 'con'.

The search command finds only the first occurrence of the specified string. To continue the search for further occurrences of the same string, simply type **s** again. Thus, typing

```
*1,4sir
        1: first line of text
*s
        3: third line of text
 *_
```

causes **Edlin** to first find the string 'ir' in the word 'first' of line 1:, then by typing **s** again, it forces **Edlin** to find the same string 'ir' in the word 'third' of line 3:.

The Search & Replace Command:

This command is similar to the search command, except that it requires a replacement string. Thus, typing

```
*1,4r edited^Z re-edited
```

will cause all occurrences of the word 'edited' to be replaced by the word 're-edited' in the specified lines. Here, of course, it only occurs once in line 2: of the text. The character ^Z is the two-key depression Ctrl+Z which acts as a delimiter between the two strings. Again note that the space in front of both words becomes part of both the searching and the replacing strings.

The Transfer Command:

This command transfers the contents of a file into the file currently being edited. The format of the command is:

[n] T filespec

where

n   specifies the line number where the new data is to be inserted. The data is inserted before the specified line. If the line number is omitted, then the current line is used.

filespec specifies the file that you want to insert the contents of into the current file in memory.

Exiting Edlin

To end the current session and exit **Edlin** at any point, type

*e

which saves a new file under the chosen filename.

However, if the filename already existed on disc prior to using **Edlin**, ending **Edlin** has the following effect:

First the name of the old file on the disc is given the extension .bak, then the new file you have created by editing the old one is saved with the original extension. In this way you can make mistakes without disastrous effects since the system makes a back-up file of the original. If need be, you could delete the .txt file and then rename the back-up file (.bak) to its original name and extension.

Note that **Edlin** is disciplined not to allow editing of back-up files so, should you want to start using **Edlin** to edit the contents of a .bak file, you must first rename it, by giving it a different extension, before proceeding.

If, on the other hand, you realised that too many mistakes were made during editing, you could use the **q** command to quit, as follows:

*q

instead of using the **e** command as discussed above. Doing this causes **Edlin** to ask you whether you want to abort. Typing **y** (for yes), leaves the name and contents of the original file on disc unaltered.

120

INDEX

122

NOTES

NOTES

NOTES

NOTES

NOTES